THE WAFFLE COOKBOOK

BY
LESLIE FREIBERGER

ILLUSTRATED BY STEPHANIE DONON

HPBooks

DEDICATION

To my husband Benjie—who makes all my dreams come true. Thanks for giving me my first waffle iron.

ACKNOWLEGMENTS

Special thanks to Mom, Dad, Shirley, Freddy, Colleen, Jeanne and Deborah for all your help and always saying four very important little words . . . "You can do it!" Thank you to all my family and friends, especially Lisa, Scott, Marlee, Ryan, Kyle, Joe and Lisa for the use of your taste buds, your great suggestions and support. To Larry, Nick and Laura, thanks for taking a chance and the vote of confidence. And to my guardian angels—Nanny, Grandma and Bruce, who continue to inspire.

HPBooks
are published by
The Berkley Publishing Group
200 Madison Avenue
New York, NY 10016
© 1992 Leslie Freiberger
Illustration © 1992 Price Stern Sloan, Inc.

Library of Congress Cataloging-in-Publication Data

Freiberger, Leslie.
   Waffles / by Leslie Freiberger.
   p. cm.
   Includes index.
   ISBN 1-55788-036-0
   1. Pancakes, waffles, etc. I. Title.
TX770.P34F75 1992
91-47000   641.8'15—dc20
                      CIP

Printed in the United States of America
10 9 8 7 6 5 4 3

Notice: The information in this book is true and complete to the best of our knowledge. All recommendations are made without guarantees on the part of the authors or the publisher. The authors and publisher disclaim all liability in connection with the use of this information.

This book is printed on acid-free paper.

CONTENTS

ALL ABOUT WAFFLES...

I have written this book simply because I love waffles! I still have wonderful childhood memories of waking up snuggled under a warm Hudson Bay blanket to the smell of waffles cooking. I would scamper happily down the stairs to see the steam escaping from the sides of the waffle iron, the batter resting in a large ceramic bowl, and two small saucepans on the stove. One had butter melting and the other had a bottle of syrup heating in boiling water. And smiling from ear to ear I would announce, "Oh wow, waffles!" But as I grew older I wanted more. Packaged mixes just weren't satisfying my more sophisticated palate. That is why I started experimenting with different ways of enhancing simple batters. As a result I was able to compile this collection of my favorite recipes that you can share with your family and friends.

So open your senses to this wonderful new culinary experience. Toss aside your preconceptions of ordinary waffles with butter and syrup and replace it with these waffles which are crisp, colorful, flavorful and remarkably aromatic. Now you can proudly serve waffles not only for breakfast and brunch, but for lunch or dinner as the main dish, a side dish or dessert. This book presents a cornucopia of delicious new tastes and textures never before thought of in relationship to a waffle. Imaginative variations of old favorite batter recipes now incorporate pureed fruits and vegetables, natural grains, spices and nuts directly into the batter, not just on top, to create a nutritious foundation for any meal of the day. Using cookie cutters or cutting the waffles into quarters or wedges, a new creative style of decorating and serving can be accomplished. In other words it's time for waffles to come out of the breakfast nook and into the dining room!

Waffles were first introduced to America in 1796 by the Dutch. And as legend has it, waffles date back as far as the Middle Ages where they were enjoyed throughout Brussels (of course prepared on Belgian waffle irons). The Pennsylvania Dutch are credited with inventing the heart-shaped waffle iron. It wasn't until the 1950s that the waffle reached the height of its popularity in the United States.

Waffles can now be included in the new American way of cooking, dining and entertaining. Breakfast has become the day's rushed or forgotten meal, usually just a cup of coffee. While on the other hand, brunch is a relaxing way of spending time with family and friends. The recipes in the breakfast and brunch chapter offer many wonderful possibilities to turn both these morning meals into a celebration. For lunch, subtle flavored batters enhance chilled salads and even hot burgers. For delightfully different dinners, batters with natural grains were developed to serve as foundations for saucy main dishes like the hearty Beef Stroganoff or gourmet Shrimp Linden that are typically served over rice or noodles. And when served hot, these waffles become novel alternatives to breads, coffee cakes and dinner rolls.

Batters for the appetizer waffles can be made ahead of time, then cooked and assembled just before your guests arrive, allowing you more time to entertain instead of working in the kitchen. With the use of cookie cutters waffles have become the ultimate finger food. The dessert waffles are irresistible to everyone's sweet tooth. Imagine layer cakes, gingerbread or s'mores all made with waffles.

Don't be scared off by a long list of ingredients or the steps in cooking, because these recipes are really simple to make and waffles are extremely versatile. Feel free to mix and match batters with toppings from other recipes or create some toppings of your own. Be daring. Let your imagination be your guide. But most of all have fun! All of these recipes are designed to be enjoyable to prepare and to bring a little humor, a new taste and a little elegance to all your eating experiences. So, on behalf of all the following recipes, thanks for inviting us to your dining table and parties. And just sit back and smile when you hear, "Oh wow, waffles!".

Helpful Hints

Here are just a few things that I've learned along the way that will help you make the best waffles ever. One of the most important things to do is season the waffle iron correctly according to the manufacturer's instructions. Never scrub or scour the grids, instead lightly brush out any loose crumbs and wipe the outside with a damp sponge when you're finished.

Be careful not to over beat the batter, or your waffles will be tough, not crisp and light. Don't worry, you can leave a few, small lumps in the batter. They will dissolve during cooking. In high altitudes use about 25 percent less baking powder.

Batters can be made ahead of time and either refrigerated for a day or two or frozen for a longer period of time. Before cooking, bring batter to room temperature, stir slightly and prepare according to the recipe. Cooked waffles can also be frozen and reheated in either the toaster or microwave oven and still maintain their rich flavor.

Preheat the waffle iron for a few minutes or until it's hot enough that a few drops of water will bounce around on the surface of the grids. It's best with all the batters to push them to within about 1 inch of the edges of the waffle iron with a wooden spoon or spatula. This will allow them to cook more evenly. Most manufacturers recommend cooking waffles until the steam stops escaping from the edges and/or the red indicator light on the top goes out. This is not always the best way. Because some of these batters are heavier than traditional batters they might take a minute or two longer to cook. If the lid resists when you try to raise it, the waffles are not quite ready. They are finished when you can easily open the lid, and they are crisp and golden-brown, usually around 4 or 5 minutes. The first waffles may take longer to cook than the remaining waffles. Even though waffles are best served right from the waffle iron, they can still be kept warm in the oven up to 15 to 20 minutes without any negative effects. Any longer than that they could either become dried or soggy. Do not stack waffles because that will also make them soggy and soft. Waffles cool fast, so serve them on warm plates. You can keep plates warm in the oven with the finished waffles until you're ready to serve them.

What about the scraps—those odd shaped leftover pieces that remain after using a cookie cutter? Because nothing should go to waste, you can create croutons by cutting these into smaller pieces and lightly browning them in butter and garlic. Let cool thoroughly and they become the perfect accent to soups and salads. Bread crumbs can be created by processing leftover waffles in a blender or food processor. And finally, dessert waffle crumbs can be mixed with softened butter and pressed into a pie pan for a delightfully new and delicious pie crust.

Equipment

These batters were developed for, and tested in traditional 8-inch square or 6-inch round waffle irons. But they can easily be cooked in any kind of speciality waffle iron as well. Waffle irons with stylized grids offer great patterns that can enhance the design of a finished waffle. Just be careful how much batter you pour in, and remember that your finished waffle count may vary. Be sure to follow the manufacturer's instructions for the waffle iron you are using; each company's printed material will differ slightly . When the waffle iron is on be aware that it is hot. Choose a solid surface that won't stain and is easy to clean to set up your cooking area. A tile counter or stove top is the best. And of course, always keep small children at a distance so they won't get burned.

Ingredients

Almond Butter: This spread is similar to peanut butter in consistency, but it's made with fresh ground almonds instead of peanuts. It is available at natural food stores and gourmet markets.

Butter: The rich texture and delicious taste of butter enhances the flavor of the waffles. You can substitute margarine for butter if necessary.

Chocolate: Follow the recipes exactly and use only the type of chocolate specified. Do not substitute one type of chocolate for another; they all have very distinctive characteristics. Semisweet chocolate is similar to bittersweet chocolate, and their sweetness varies according to the brand. Always be sure to use real chocolate, not an imitation.

Eggs: I suggest using Grade AA large or extra-large eggs. They will give the batter the volume necessary for perfect waffles. If large eggs are unavailable, you can use two small eggs to one large egg. When eggs are separated and the egg whites are beaten and folded into the batter, they make the finished waffles crisper. Be careful not to let any of the egg yolk mix in with the egg white, it can prevent the white from whipping and peaking properly.

Extracts: There is a variety of extracts used throughout these recipes, all of which are available in most markets. Always use pure extracts and not imitations; the taste difference is remarkable.

Flours: Each of the flours included in this book possesses a unique flavor specifically chosen for that recipe. Do not substitute cake flour or self-rising flour for all-purpose flour. Unbleached all-purpose flour has more flavor than bleached flour. All of the speciality flours are available in natural food stores and gourmet markets.

Fruit: Whenever possible it's best to use fresh, ripe fruit. If a fruit is not available fresh, then substitute thawed frozen fruit. Canned fruit, unless specified in a recipe, should not be substituted because it usually does not have the same flavor and texture.

Herbs & Spices: When using dried herbs and spices, buy small amounts and restock frequently. After a short amount of time, even dried herbs and spices have a tendency to loose their true flavor.

Nuts: All the nuts have been chosen to blend with the batter's flavor. But if you don't like that specific nut flavor, feel free to substitute or omit any nut. Store nuts in the refrigerator or freezer; they become rancid quickly.

Milk: Whole milk is best in these batters, but low-fat milk can be substituted. I don't recommend using non-fat or skim milk, because you will not have the same results.

Oil: All flavorless vegetable oils are similar and can be used in the batters. Do not substitute other flavored oils unless specified in the recipe.

Shortening: I prefer shortening instead of oil to grease the grids, because it's easier to brush on and doesn't leave any residue on the finished waffles. If you prefer to use oil, brush on sparingly.

Unsweetened Cocoa Powder: Don't confuse cocoa powder with hot chocolate mix. Unsweetened cocoa powder has the rich flavor of chocolate without the sugar.

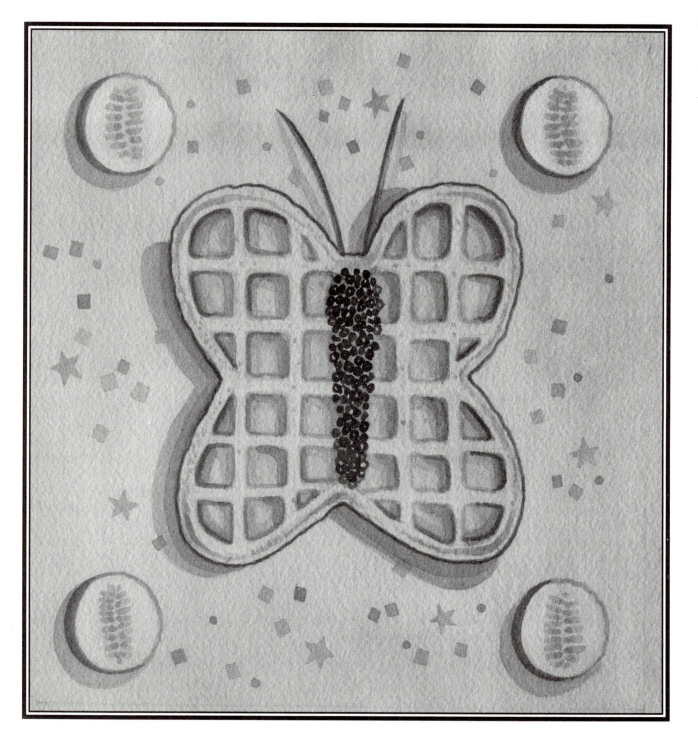

APPETIZERS

Open your mind to this novel idea for waffles. Out-of-the-ordinary, flavored, full-size waffles are cut into bite-size rounds and finished with delectable toppings, creating an enchanting finger food. Perfect for when friends and family get together, or to start off even the most elegant of evenings.

Green Clouds Over a Blue Moon

This is a fun name for blue cornmeal waffle rounds with guacamole. Fresh and flavorful, the blue and green colors make these waffles a playful appetizer. And of course you can enjoy these more often than just once in a blue moon!

1 cup blue cornmeal
1 cup all-purpose flour
1 tablespoon baking powder
1/2 teaspoon baking soda
1/4 teaspoon salt
2 eggs, separated
1-3/4 cups buttermilk
2 tablespoons light brown sugar
1/4 cup vegetable oil
Vegetable shortening or oil for grids

GUACAMOLE:

3 avocados
2 tablespoons fresh lemon juice
1 garlic clove, minced
1 tomato, diced
1 small onion, chopped
2 tablespoons dairy sour cream
2 tablespoons chopped cilantro
1/4 teaspoon salt
1/4 teaspoon pepper
Spicy salsa to taste

Prepare Guacamole. Preheat waffle iron. In a medium-size bowl whisk together blue cornmeal, all-purpose flour, baking powder, baking soda and salt. In a large bowl beat together egg yolks, buttermilk, brown sugar and oil. Gradually stir in cornmeal mixture. Beat until smooth. In a small bowl whip egg whites until soft peaks are formed. Fold into batter. Lightly brush hot grids with shortening or oil. Pour enough batter to fill two-thirds of the waffle iron. Cook until crisp and a golden-blue color. Cool finished waffles on a rack. Repeat with the remaining batter. To serve, cut finished waffles into 2-inch rounds with a cookie cutter. Place about 1 tablespoon Guacamole on top of each round. Makes about 4 waffles or 25 rounds.

GUACAMOLE

Remove the pits from the avocados and set aside. In a medium-size bowl mash avocados with a fork. Stir in lemon juice, garlic, tomato, onion, sour cream, cilantro, salt, pepper and salsa until combined. Place a pit on top to retard darkening. Cover with plastic wrap. Keep refrigerated until ready to serve. If Guacamole turns dark on the surface stir in 1 additional tablespoon fresh lemon juice. Makes about 2 cups.

Pizza on Sourdough Waffles

Cut into rounds, these miniature pizzas taste as though they just came out of a pizza oven. The unique taste of the sourdough is truly worth all of the effort, but remember if you're starting from scratch allow two to three days. If you don't have the time, then you can substitute the Crispy Waffles (page 66).

Sourdough Waffles (page 25)
1/2 cup finely chopped onion
1/2 cup finely chopped yellow bell pepper
8 ounces pepperoni, thinly sliced
2 cups shredded mozzarella cheese (8 ounces)
1/2 cup chopped olives
Crushed red pepper (optional)

PIZZA SAUCE:

1/4 cup olive oil
1 garlic clove, minced
1-1/2 cups Italian plum tomato puree
1/2 cup tomato paste
1-1/2 teaspoons chopped fresh basil
1-1/2 teaspoons chopped fresh oregano
1 teaspoon sugar

Prepare waffles according to directions on page 25. Prepare Pizza Sauce. Preheat broiler. Cut finished waffles into 2-inch rounds with a cookie cutter. Place on a baking sheet. On each round spread about 2 tablespoons of the hot sauce. Top with onion, bell pepper, pepperoni, cheese and olives. For a spicy pizza sprinkle with crushed red pepper. Place under the broiler just until cheese has melted, 3 to 4 minutes. Serve immediately. Makes about 4 waffles or 24 pizza rounds.

PIZZA SAUCE

In a medium-size saucepan heat olive oil over low heat. Add garlic and cook until soft. Add tomato puree, tomato paste, basil, oregano and sugar. Stir until smooth. Increase heat to medium and bring sauce to a boil. Reduce the heat. Keep sauce warm until ready to use, stirring occasionally. Makes about 1-1/2 cups.

Shirley's Spicy Southwestern Waffle Rounds

Named for my mom-in-law who helped me create them in her gourmet kitchen, these waffles are always a great hit at parties. Don't be intimidated by the long list of ingredients, the waffles are actually easy to make and they look and taste great.

2 tablespoons olive oil
1 cup grated zucchini
1/2 cup chopped green bell pepper
1 garlic clove, minced
1 cup all-purpose flour
1 cup yellow cornmeal
1 tablespoon baking powder
1/4 teaspoon baking soda
1/4 teaspoon onion powder
1/2 teaspoon salt
1/4 teaspoon pepper
1/2 cup milk

1 (17-oz.) can creamed corn
2 eggs
1/4 cup butter, melted, cooled
1 tablespoon maple syrup
2 or 3 tablespoons chopped jalapeño peppers
1 tablespoon chopped cilantro
1 tablespoon chopped parsley
1/2 cup grated Parmesan cheese (1-1/2 ounces)
Vegetable shortening or oil for grids
3/4 cup dairy sour cream
1/4 cup salsa

In a medium-size skillet heat olive oil over medium-low heat. Add zucchini, bell pepper and garlic. Cook until soft, 2 to 3 minutes. Remove from heat. Preheat waffle iron. Preheat oven to 250°F (120°C). In a medium-size bowl sift together all-purpose flour, cornmeal, baking powder, baking soda, onion powder, salt and pepper. In a large bowl beat together milk, creamed corn, eggs, butter and maple syrup. Gradually stir in flour mixture. Beat until smooth. Add jalapeño peppers, cilantro, parsley, cheese and cooked vegetables. Stir until all ingredients are blended. Batter will be thick. Lightly brush hot grids with shortening or oil. Pour enough batter to fill two-thirds of the waffle iron. Push batter to the edges with a wooden spoon. Cook until crisp and golden-brown. Cut finished waffles into 2-inch rounds with a cookie cutter. Place waffle rounds in the oven on a rack to keep warm until ready to serve. Serve warm with sour cream and salsa on top of each round. Makes about 3 waffles or 20 rounds.

Creamed Spinach Waffles

As a hot hors d'oeuvre these waffle rounds are ideal! Serve them proudly at the most elegant of dinner parties and delight all of your guests with the delicious taste.

1-1/2 pounds fresh spinach, rinsed well
1/4 cup water
1/3 cup milk
1/3 cup dairy sour cream
3 tablespoons grated Parmesan cheese
1/4 teaspoon ground nutmeg
1/2 teaspoon salt
1/4 teaspoon pepper
1 teaspoon sugar

2 eggs, separated
3 tablespoons butter, melted, cooled
1/2 cup all-purpose flour
1/2 cup oat flour
1 tablespoon baking powder
1/2 teaspoon baking soda
2 tablespoons pine nuts
Vegetable shortening or oil for grids
1 cup dairy sour cream

Preheat waffle iron. Preheat oven to 250°F (120°C). In a large saucepan combine spinach and water. Cover and cook 3 to 4 minutes until wilted. Drain. In a blender or food processor fitted with the metal blade combine cooked spinach, milk, the 1/3 cup sour cream, cheese, nutmeg, salt, pepper and sugar. Process until smooth. Transfer to a large bowl. Add egg yolks and butter. In a medium-size bowl sift together all-purpose flour, oat flour, baking powder and baking soda. Gradually stir into spinach mixture. Beat until smooth. Stir in pine nuts. In a small bowl whip egg whites until soft peaks are formed. Fold into batter. Lightly brush hot grids with shortening or oil. Pour enough batter to fill two-thirds of the waffle iron. Cook until crisp and golden-brown. Cut finished waffles into 2-inch rounds with a cookie cutter. Place waffle rounds in the oven on a rack to keep warm until ready to serve. Repeat with the remaining batter. Place about 1 tablespoon sour cream on top of each round and serve immediately. Makes about 2 waffles or 15 rounds.

Ceviche on Sweet Potato Waffles

Ideal to serve at any gathering, the combination of the spicy appetizer and the subtle sweet flavor of the waffles is unforgettable.

1 pound sweet potatoes
1 cup all-purpose flour
1/2 cup whole-wheat pastry flour
1 tablespoon baking powder
1/4 teaspoon baking soda
1 teaspoon ground nutmeg
1/4 teaspoon salt
2 eggs
1-1/2 cups buttermilk
1/4 cup butter, melted, cooled
1/2 teaspoon almond extract
1/2 cup packed dark brown sugar
Vegetable shortening or oil for grids

CEVICHE:

1 cup fresh lime juice
3/4 cup fresh lemon juice
3/4 pound fresh red snapper, cut into 1/2-inch pieces
1/4 cup tequila
1 garlic clove, minced
2 tablespoons grated orange zest
1 tablespoon sugar
1 teaspoon salt
3 medium-size serrano chile peppers, finely chopped
2 yellow chile peppers, chopped
5 green onions, chopped
1 cup cooked whole-kernel corn
1 red bell pepper, diced
1/2 cup chopped cilantro leaves

Prepare the Ceviche. Preheat oven to 450°F (230°C). Pierce sweet potatoes several times with a fork. Place on a baking sheet. Bake until tender 45 to 55 minutes. Or place sweet potatoes on a microwave-safe plate with 2 tablespoons of water. Cover with plastic wrap and cook in a microwave oven until tender 10 to 12 minutes. Cool. Peel sweet potatoes, place in a small bowl and mash with a fork. Set aside. Preheat waffle iron. Preheat oven to 250°F (120°C). In a medium-size bowl sift together all-purpose flour, pastry flour, baking powder, baking soda, nutmeg and salt. In a large bowl beat together eggs, buttermilk, butter, almond extract and brown sugar. Gradually stir in flour mixture. Beat until smooth. Stir in mashed sweet potatoes. Batter will be thick. Lightly brush hot grids with shortening or oil. Pour enough batter to fill two-thirds of the waffle iron. Push batter to the edges with a wooden spoon. Cook until crisp and golden-brown. Cut finished waffles into 2-inch rounds with a cookie cutter. Keep finished waffles warm in the oven on a rack until ready to serve. To serve, with a slotted spoon place chilled Ceviche on top of each round. Makes about 3 waffles or 20 rounds.

CEVICHE

In a large bowl combine lime juice and lemon juice. Stir in red snapper pieces; cover. Set aside 1-1/2 hours. In a medium-size bowl combine tequila, garlic, orange zest, sugar, salt, serrano chile peppers, yellow chile peppers, green onions, corn, red bell pepper and cilantro. Add to red snapper. Stir until all ingredients are combined. Cover tightly with plastic wrap, and refrigerate 8 hours.

Bread Crumb Waffles with Sautéed Mushrooms

Sophisticated enough for a dinner party and simple enough for just a casual get-together with friends, these waffles are a wonderful way to kick-off your evening.

1-1/4 cups dry plain bread crumbs
1 cup all-purpose flour
1 tablespoon baking powder
1/2 teaspoon baking soda
1/4 teaspoon salt
1/2 teaspoon dried leaf basil
1/2 teaspoon dried leaf oregano
1/4 teaspoon dried leaf tarragon
3 eggs, separated
1/2 cup dairy sour cream
1-3/4 cups milk
1/3 cup vegetable oil
Vegetable shortening or oil for grids
1/4 cup grated Parmesan cheese (3/4 ounce)

SAUTÉED MUSHROOMS:

30 small mushrooms
1/4 cup olive oil
2 medium-size shallots, finely diced
2 garlic cloves, minced
2 tablespoons butter
1/2 teaspoon dried leaf tarragon
1/4 teaspoon dried leaf sage
1/4 teaspoon pepper
1 tablespoon chopped parsley
2 tablespoons dry white wine

Preheat waffle iron. Preheat oven to 250°F (120°C). In a medium-size bowl whisk together bread crumbs, flour, baking powder, baking soda, salt, basil, oregano and tarragon. In a large bowl beat together egg yolks, sour cream, milk and oil. Gradually stir in bread crumb mixture. Beat until smooth. In a small bowl whip egg whites until soft peaks are formed. Fold into batter. Batter will be thick. Lightly brush hot grids with shortening or oil. Pour enough batter to fill two-thirds of the waffle iron. Push batter to the edges with a wooden spoon. Cook until crisp and golden-brown. While waffles are cooking, prepare Sautéed Mushrooms. Keep finished waffles warm in the oven on a rack until ready to serve. Repeat with the remaining batter. To serve, cut finished waffles into 1-inch rounds with a cookie cutter. Remove the mushrooms one at a time with a spoon and place flat-side down on top of each waffle round. Drizzle the remaining oil and herb mixture over each mushroom. Sprinkle with Parmesan cheese. Serve immediately. Makes about 3 waffles or 30 rounds.

SAUTÉED MUSHROOMS

From each mushroom remove the stem and cut the bottom to flatten surface. In a large skillet heat oil over low heat. Add shallots and garlic; cook, stirring, 1 minute. Stir in butter, tarragon, sage, pepper, parsley and wine. Add mushrooms. Sauté mushrooms, turning constantly until completely coated with oil and herbs, about 5 minutes. Cover and keep warm until ready to serve.

Pink Butterflies

Yuck, beets! This is one of the reasons why these are called Pink Butterflies and because, like a beautiful butterfly evolving from its ugly cocoon, these beautiful, delicious treats evolve from the lowly beet. The trick is not to let anyone know the true contents until after they've proclaimed, "These are my favorites!"

6 medium-size beets, cut into quarters
1/3 cup milk
1 cup all-purpose flour
1 cup oat flour
1-1/2 tablespoons baking powder
1 teaspoon baking soda
3/4 teaspoon salt
1-1/2 teaspoons pepper
1-1/2 teaspoons onion powder
1/4 cup sugar
2 eggs, separated
1/2 cup dairy sour cream

1/2 cup buttermilk
1 tablespoon maple syrup
1 tablespoon white wine vinegar
1/3 cup vegetable oil
3 tablespoons chopped fresh dill
Vegetable shortening or oil for grids

BUTTERFLY TOPPING:

1/2 cup dairy sour cream
1/4 cup beet puree (from above)
1 (2-oz.) jar inexpensive black caviar
1 cucumber, cut in lengthwise wedges for garnish

Place beets in a large saucepan with enough water to cover. Boil until tender, 20 to 30 minutes. Drain. Cool cooked beets under cold water and peel. In a blender or food processor fitted with the metal blade combine cooked beets and milk. Process until smooth. Set aside. In a medium-size bowl sift together all-purpose flour, oat flour, baking powder, baking soda, salt, pepper, onion powder and sugar. In a large bowl beat together egg yolks, sour cream, buttermilk, maple syrup, vinegar and oil. Add 3/4 cup of beet puree. Set the remaining puree aside for the topping. Gradually stir in flour mixture. Beat until smooth. Stir in dill. In a small bowl whip egg whites until soft peaks are formed. Fold into batter. Batter will be thick. Preheat waffle iron. Lightly brush hot grids with shortening or oil. Pour enough batter to fill two-thirds of the waffle iron. Push batter to the edges with a wooden spoon. Cook until crisp and golden-brown. Cool finished waffles on a rack a few minutes. Cut with a butterfly cookie cutter. Prepare Butterfly Topping. To serve, spread a thin layer of Butterfly Topping over each waffle butterfly. With a knife, place a line of caviar down the center to look like a butterfly body. Garnish the serving tray with cucumber wedges. Makes about 3 waffles or 12 butterflies.

BUTTERFLY TOPPING

In a medium-size bowl combine sour cream and remaining 1/4 cup beet puree. Keep refrigerated until ready to serve. Makes about 3/4 cup.

Waffle-dillas!

When everyone is sitting around watching a sporting event and screaming for something other than chips 'n' dip, surprise them with this zesty, tasty treat. Similar to the Mexican favorite, the quesadilla, this hot appetizer is a winner!

1 cup white cornmeal
1/2 cup all-purpose flour
1 tablespoon baking powder
1/2 teaspoon baking soda
1/2 teaspoon salt
2 tablespoons sugar
2 eggs, separated
1/4 cup dairy sour cream
1-1/4 cups buttermilk
1/3 cup peanut oil
Vegetable shortening or oil for grids

CHEESE TOPPING:

2 cups shredded Monterey jack cheese (8 ounces)
2 teaspoons diced jalapeño peppers with seeds
2 tablespoons diced green chiles
3 tablespoons chopped cilantro

Preheat waffle iron. In a medium-size bowl sift together cornmeal, flour, baking powder, baking soda, salt and sugar. In a large bowl beat together egg yolks, sour cream, buttermilk and oil. Gradually stir in cornmeal mixture. Beat until smooth. In a small bowl whip egg whites until soft peaks are formed. Fold into batter. Lightly brush hot grids with shortening or oil. Pour enough batter to fill two-thirds of the waffle iron. Cook until crisp and golden-brown. While waffles are cooking, prepare Cheese Topping and preheat the broiler. Cool finished waffles on a rack. Repeat with the remaining batter. Cover finished waffles with Cheese Topping. Place under the broiler just long enough to melt the cheese. With a knife cut into 2-inch pieces. Serve immediately. Makes about 2 waffles or 6 servings.

CHEESE TOPPING

In a medium-size bowl combine cheese, jalapeño peppers, green chiles and cilantro. Makes about 2 cups.

Zesty Corn Bread Waffle Rounds with Rainbow Relish

Because these waffles are both delicious and colorful, they're the perfect beginning to any Southwestern meal. Best of all everything can be made ahead of time to allow the host more time to be with the guests.

1 cup yellow cornmeal
1 cup all-purpose flour
1 tablespoon baking powder
1/4 teaspoon baking soda
1/4 teaspoon salt
1 tablespoon sugar
2 eggs
1-3/4 cups buttermilk
1/3 cup butter, melted, cooled
1/2 cup diced red bell pepper
2 tablespoons minced cilantro
1/2 cup diced red onion
2 tablespoons diced mild green chiles

1/2 teaspoon dried sage leaves
Vegetable shortening or oil for grids

RAINBOW RELISH:
1 (16-oz.) can whole-kernel corn, drained
1/2 red onion, finely chopped
1 green bell pepper, finely chopped
1 red bell pepper, finely chopped
1/2 cup raspberry vinegar
1 tablespoon sugar
1 teaspoon salt
1/2 teaspoon pepper
1/2 teaspoon dry mustard
1 cup fresh raspberries

Prepare Rainbow Relish. Preheat waffle iron. Preheat oven to 250°F (120°C). In a medium-size bowl sift together cornmeal, all-purpose flour, baking powder, baking soda, salt and sugar. In a large bowl beat together egg yolks, buttermilk and butter. Gradually stir in cornmeal mixture. Beat until smooth. Add red bell pepper, cilantro, red onion, green chiles and sage. Stir until all ingredients are combined. Lightly brush hot grids with shortening or oil. Pour enough batter to fill two-thirds of the waffle iron. Cook until crisp and golden-brown. Keep finished waffles warm in the oven on a rack until ready to serve. To serve, cut finished waffles into 2-inch rounds with a cookie cutter. Spoon chilled Rainbow Relish on top of each waffle round. Serve immediately. Makes about 3 waffles or 20 rounds.

RAINBOW RELISH

In a medium-size saucepan combine corn, red onion, green bell pepper, red bell pepper, vinegar, sugar, salt, pepper and dry mustard. Bring to a boil. Reduce the heat and simmer 30 minutes. Stir occasionally. Relish will thicken. Set aside to cool. Stir in raspberries. Chill 2 hours before serving.

Zucchini Waffle Rounds

This is a terrific, hot hors d'oeuvre, that is quick to make, easy to serve and surprisingly delicious. Of course they are healthful too, but no one needs to know that!

1/4 cup olive oil
1 garlic clove, minced
2 cups grated zucchini
1-1/2 cups all-purpose flour
1 tablespoon baking powder
1/4 teaspoon baking soda
1/4 teaspoon onion powder

1/4 teaspoon salt
1/4 teaspoon pepper
2 eggs, separated
1 cup milk
1/4 cup dairy sour cream
Vegetable shortening or oil for grids
1/2 cup grated Parmesan cheese

In a small skillet slowly heat olive oil over low heat. Add garlic and zucchini; sauté 1 minute. Remove from heat. Preheat waffle iron. Preheat oven to 250°F (120°C). In a medium-size bowl sift together flour, baking powder, baking soda, onion powder, salt and pepper. In a large bowl beat together egg yolks, milk and sour cream. Gradually stir in flour mixture. Beat until smooth. Stir sautéed zucchini into batter. In a small bowl whip egg whites until soft peaks are formed. Fold into batter. Lightly brush hot grids with shortening or oil. Pour enough batter to fill two-thirds of the waffle iron. Cook until crisp and golden-brown. Keep finished waffles warm in the oven on a rack until ready to serve. Repeat with the remaining batter. To serve, cut finished waffles into 1-inch rounds with a cookie cutter. Sprinkle Parmesan cheese on top of each round. Serve immediately. Makes about 3 waffles or 30 rounds.

Doggie Waffles

These waffles are specially designed for your furry four-legged family members. Finally fresh, nutritious dog treats—it's a dog's life!

1 cup all-purpose flour
1 cup whole-wheat flour
1 teaspoon baking powder
2 eggs
1-1/2 cups beef broth

3 tablespoons vegetable oil
1 garlic clove, minced
1 cup shredded mild Cheddar cheese (4 ounces)
Vegetable shortening or oil for grids

Preheat waffle iron. In a medium-size bowl sift together all-purpose flour, whole-wheat flour and baking powder. In a large bowl beat together eggs, beef broth, oil and garlic. Gradually stir in flour mixture. Beat until smooth. Stir in Cheddar cheese. Lightly brush hot grids with shortening or oil. Pour enough batter to fill two-thirds of the waffle iron. Cook until crisp and golden-brown. Place finished waffles on a rack. While the waffles are still warm cut with a dog bone shaped cookie cutter or cut into 1-inch squares. Repeat with the remaining batter. Let waffles cool thoroughly before serving. Makes about 4 waffles or about 25 dog bones.

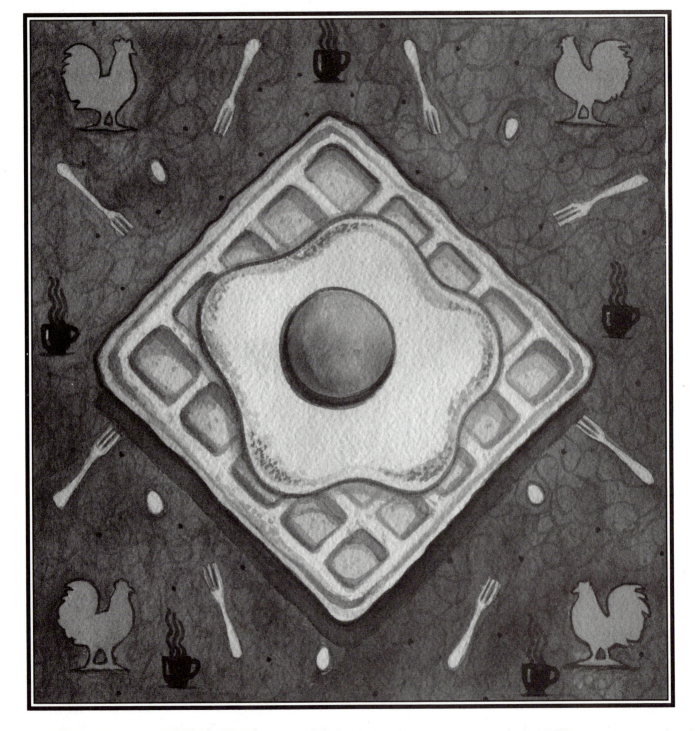

BREAKFAST & BRUNCH

There's nothing better in the morning than the aroma of waffles cooking and fresh coffee brewing. These eye-opening recipes are guaranteed to wake up anyone's appetite. Now it's quick and easy to whip up a hot, fresh gourmet breakfast, or a late morning brunch. These waffles have everything you need to get your day started with a smile.

Apple Mint Waffles with Sautéed Apples

This waffle is extra-ordinary. Perfect for brunches because it looks pretty and smells inviting with just a hint of mint. Serve with the mint sprigs around the plate or platter for a beautiful presentation.

1 cup coarsely chopped Red Delicious apples
1 tablespoon lemon juice
1-1/2 cups all-purpose flour
1/2 cup oat flour
1 tablespoon baking powder
1/4 teaspoon baking soda
2 eggs, separated
1-1/2 cups milk
1/4 cup plain low-fat yogurt
1 teaspoon mint extract
1/2 cup packed light brown sugar

1/2 cup butter, melted, cooled
1/3 cup slivered almonds
Vegetable shortening or oil for grids
Powdered sugar
Fresh mint sprigs for garnish

SAUTÉED APPLES:

4 Red Delicious apples
1/2 cup butter
2 tablespoons light brown sugar

Preheat waffle iron. Preheat oven to 250°F (120°C). Toss chopped apple with lemon juice. Set aside. In a medium-size bowl sift together all-purpose flour, oat flour, baking powder and baking soda. In a large bowl beat together egg yolks, milk, yogurt, mint extract, brown sugar and butter. Gradually stir in flour mixture. Beat until smooth. Stir in almonds and chopped apple. In a small bowl whip egg whites until soft peaks are formed. Fold into batter. Lightly brush hot grids with shortening or oil. Pour enough batter to fill two-thirds of the waffle iron. Cook until crisp and golden-brown. While the waffles are cooking, prepare the Sautéed Apples. Keep finished waffles warm in the oven on a rack until ready to serve. Repeat with the remaining batter. To serve, remove Sautéed Apple slices one at a time from the skillet with a spatula. Place on top of finished waffles. Do not stack or overlap slices. With a spoon drip sugar sauce over the apples. Sift powdered sugar over waffles. Garnish with fresh mint sprigs. Makes about 4 waffles or 4 servings.

SAUTÉED APPLES

Cut apples into quarters; remove cores. Thinly slice apples. In a large skillet melt butter over low heat. Lightly sauté apple slices 2 to 3 minutes on both sides until light brown. Sprinkle brown sugar over the top. Allow sugar to dissolve into the butter. Keep warm until ready to serve.

Orange Spice Waffles

These warm and sunny waffles with just the essence of orange and spices are a great way to get your morning started, especially Mondays!

1 cup whole-wheat flour
1 cup all-purpose flour
1 tablespoon baking powder
1/2 teaspoon baking soda
1 teaspoon ground nutmeg
1 teaspoon ground cinnamon
2 eggs, separated
3/4 cup orange juice
1 cup milk
1/2 cup buttermilk

1/3 cup butter, melted, cooled
1/2 teaspoon dark molasses
1 tablespoon orange extract
1/3 cup packed light brown sugar
2 tablespoons grated orange zest
1/2 cup orange marmalade
Vegetable shortening or oil for grids
1 cup butter, melted
1 cup maple syrup, warmed

Preheat waffle iron. Preheat oven to 250°F (120°C). In a medium-size bowl sift together whole-wheat flour, all-purpose flour, baking powder, baking soda, nutmeg and cinnamon. In a large bowl beat together egg yolks, orange juice, milk, buttermilk, 1/3 cup butter, molasses, orange extract and brown sugar. Gradually stir in flour mixture. Beat until smooth. Stir in orange zest and marmalade. In a small bowl whip egg whites until soft peaks are formed. Fold into batter. Lightly brush hot grids with shortening or oil. Pour enough batter to fill two-thirds of the waffle iron. Cook until crisp and golden-brown. Keep finished waffles warm in the oven on a rack until ready to serve. Serve waffles hot with melted butter and warm maple syrup. Makes about 4 waffles or 4 servings.

Pear Waffles

These waffles are lovely to serve for breakfast or brunch. Sift just a touch of powdered sugar over the top to thoroughly enjoy the subtle sweetness of the pears.

1/4 cup butter
1/2 cup packed dark brown sugar
1/4 teaspoon ground ginger
2 cups all-purpose flour
1-1/2 tablespoons baking powder
1/4 teaspoon salt
2 eggs

1 cup milk
1/2 cup plain low-fat yogurt
1 teaspoon vanilla extract
1 cup diced peeled Anjou pears tossed with 1
    tablespoon lemon juice
Vegetable shortening or oil for grids
Powdered sugar

Preheat waffle iron. Preheat oven to 250°F (120°C). In a small saucepan melt butter over low heat. Add brown sugar and ginger. Stir constantly until sugar is thoroughly dissolved. Keep warm until ready to add to batter. In a medium-size bowl sift together flour, baking powder and salt. In a large bowl beat together eggs, milk, yogurt and vanilla. Gradually stir in flour mixture. Beat until smooth. Stir in melted butter mixture and pears. Lightly brush hot grids with shortening or oil. Pour enough batter to fill two-thirds of the waffle iron. Cook until crisp and golden-brown. Keep finished waffles warm in the oven until ready to serve. Repeat with the remaining batter. Sift powdered sugar over the waffles. Makes about 4 waffles or 4 servings.

Eggs Benedict on Sourdough Waffles

The secret to great eggs Benedict is timing. Simply follow this schedule: Prepare the waffles, warm the Canadian bacon, steam the asparagus, poach the eggs and start the Hollandaise Sauce. Assemble all the pieces and you're ready to go. Sourdough was perfected by pioneers who had to save batter from one baking to the next and this unique taste has been treasured ever since. Sourdough starter can be saved in the refrigerator for a long time for future uses. Even though it may seem like a lot of trouble to prepare, it's not, and it is definitely worth the time and effort. I suggest buying a package of sourdough starter in a health food store or gourmet market, because it is the easiest to prepare. The starter must be prepared two to three days ahead of time. So let's get started!

Sourdough Starter (see below)
Sourdough Waffles (see below)
6 to 8 slices Canadian bacon or thinly sliced ham
1 bunch thin asparagus, trimmed to 5-inch
  lengths
6 to 8 eggs, poached (page 25)
Hollandaise Sauce (see below)

SOURDOUGH STARTER:

1 package sourdough starter
2 cups all-purpose flour
2 cups warm water

SOURDOUGH WAFFLES:

2 cups Sourdough Starter
1-1/2 cups all-purpose flour
1 cup warm water

3 eggs, separated
1/2 cup milk
1/2 cup buttermilk
1/4 cup butter, melted, cooled
1 tablespoon sugar
1/2 teaspoon salt
1/2 teaspoon baking soda
1 tablespoon baking powder
Vegetable shortening or oil for grids

HOLLANDAISE SAUCE:

1/2 cup butter
3 egg yolks
2 tablespoons lemon juice
1/4 teaspoon salt
1/4 teaspoon white pepper
Dash of red (cayenne) pepper

Prepare starter. Prepare batter for waffles. Cook waffles. While the waffles are cooking prepare bacon, asparagus, eggs and sauce. In a large skillet cook Canadian bacon slices over low heat. Cook asparagus spears in boiling water in another large skillet 5 minutes. Reduce heat and keep warm until ready to serve. Poach the eggs (see page 25). While the eggs are poaching start to prepare the Hollandaise Sauce. To serve, cut waffles into quarter sections. Place one slice of sautéed Canadian bacon on each section. Carefully remove poached egg from the skillet with a slotted spoon and place on top of Canadian bacon. Top with 3 to 4 asparagus spears and cover with Hollandaise Sauce. Serve immediately. Makes about 4 waffles or 6 to 8 servings, 2 quarter sections per serving.

SOURDOUGH STARTER

In a large, warm bowl mix together sourdough starter, flour and warm water. With a wooden spoon stir until mixture is smooth. Cover the bowl with plastic wrap and place in a warm area 36 to 48 hours. The batter will double in size and be bubbly on top. The starter is now proofed and ready to use in recipe. Measure out needed amount. Transfer the remaining starter to a container with a tight lid. Refrigerate for future use. Before using the proofed starter again you must bring it to room temperature.

SOURDOUGH WAFFLES

In a large, warm bowl mix together starter, flour and warm water. Cover and let stand in a warm place 12 hours. After 12 hours, in a large bowl beat together egg yolks, milk, buttermilk and butter. Stir in sourdough mixture, sugar, salt, baking soda and baking powder. Beat until smooth. In a small bowl whip egg whites until soft peaks are formed. Fold into batter. Preheat waffle iron. Preheat oven to 250°F (120°C). Lightly brush hot grids with shortening or oil. Pour enough batter to fill two-thirds of the waffle iron. Cook until crisp and golden-brown. Keep finished waffles warm in the oven on a rack until ready to serve. Repeat with the remaining batter.

HOLLANDAISE SAUCE

In a small saucepan, melt butter over low heat. Keep warm without browning. In a blender combine egg yolks, lemon juice, salt, white pepper and cayenne; process on high speed a few seconds. With the blender still on, remove the lid and gradually add melted butter. The sauce is finished when all the butter is thoroughly mixed in, about 30 seconds. This sauce cannot sit, so prepare just moments before serving. Makes about 3/4 cup.

Plum Waffles with Plum Syrup

Plums are everyone's favorite summer fruit. Enjoy these sweet and tangy waffles...simply because they're plum-good!

1-1/4 cups all-purpose flour
1-1/4 cups oat flour
1-1/2 tablespoons baking powder
1/2 teaspoon baking soda
2 tablespoons granulated sugar
2 eggs, separated
1/2 cup plum preserves
1 cup buttermilk
1/4 cup orange juice
1/2 teaspoon vanilla extract

1/4 cup vegetable oil
3 medium-size firm plums, pitted, coarsely
    chopped
Vegetable shortening or oil for grids
Powdered sugar

PLUM SYRUP:
2 cups plum preserves
1/4 cup orange juice
2 tablespoons hot water
2 tablespoons creme de cassis

Preheat waffle iron. Preheat oven to 250°F (120°C). In a medium-size bowl sift together all-purpose flour, oat flour, baking powder, baking soda and granulated sugar. In a large bowl beat together egg yolks, plum preserves, buttermilk, orange juice, vanilla and oil. Gradually stir in flour mixture. Beat until smooth. Add chopped plums. In a small bowl whip egg whites until soft peaks are formed. Fold into batter. Batter will be thick. Lightly brush hot grids with shortening or oil. Pour enough batter to fill two-thirds of the waffle iron. Push batter to the edges with a wooden spoon. Cook until crisp and golden-brown. While waffles are cooking, prepare the Plum Syrup. Keep finished waffles warm in the oven on a rack until ready to serve. Repeat with the remaining batter. Serve waffles with hot Plum Syrup. Sift powdered sugar over the waffles. Makes about 4 waffles or 4 servings.

PLUM SYRUP

In a small saucepan combine plum preserves, orange juice, water and creme de cassis. Slowly warm over low heat until small bubbles appear. Simmer 2 to 3 minutes, stirring occasionally. Reduce the heat and keep warm until ready to serve. Makes about 2 cups.

Huevos Rancheros on Cornmeal Waffles

This is a zesty brunch entree. Traditionally served on a tortilla this dish becomes so much more substantial when served on hot cornmeal waffles. Everyone will love it.

1 cup yellow cornmeal
1 cup all-purpose flour
1-1/2 teaspoons baking powder
1/2 teaspoon baking soda
1/2 teaspoon salt
2 tablespoons sugar
2 cups buttermilk
2 eggs
1/4 cup vegetable oil
Vegetable shortening or oil for grids

RANCHEROS SAUCE:

2 tablespoons vegetable oil
1 medium-size onion, finely chopped

2 garlic cloves, minced
1 (28-oz.) can tomatoes, chopped
2 tablespoons tomato paste
1/4 cup medium-hot salsa
1/2 teaspoon salt
1/2 teaspoon ground oregano
1/4 cup fresh parsley, chopped

POACHED EGGS:

3 tablespoons vegetable oil
Pinch of salt
2 tablespoons vinegar
8 eggs

Prepare Rancheros Sauce. Preheat waffle iron. Preheat oven to 250°F (120°C). In a medium-size bowl sift together cornmeal, flour, baking powder, baking soda, salt and sugar. In a large bowl beat together buttermilk, eggs and oil. Gradually stir in cornmeal mixture. Beat until smooth. Lightly brush hot grids with shortening or oil. Pour enough batter to fill two-thirds of the waffle iron. Cook until crisp and light brown. Keep finished waffles warm in the oven on a rack until ready to serve. Repeat with the remaining batter. While the waffles are cooking, poach the eggs. To serve, carefully remove poached eggs with a slotted spoon placing 2 poached eggs on each waffle. Cover with hot Rancheros Sauce. Serve immediately. Makes about 4 waffles or 4 servings.

RANCHEROS SAUCE

In a medium-size, heavy saucepan slowly heat oil over low heat. Add onion and garlic. Sauté 3 to 5 minutes until softened. Add tomatoes, tomato paste, salsa, salt, oregano and parsley. Stir until all ingredients are combined. Bring to a boil. Reduce the heat and simmer 15 to 20 minutes. Stir occasionally. Keep warm until ready to serve. Makes about 2-1/2 cups.

POACHED EGGS

Grease the bottom of a large skillet with oil. Fill with enough water to cover the eggs about 1/2 inch. Add salt and vinegar. Bring water to a simmer. Break eggs into a small bowl and, one at a time, carefully slide them into the simmering water. Fit as many as eggs as possible into the skillet without crowding. If necessary repeat the process using an additional skillet. Cover and simmer 3 to 4 minutes or until the whites are firm and the yolks are still soft. Do not overcook.

Blueberry Waffles with Blueberry Sauce

This is an American classic batter recipe. Enjoy it, but remember that...roses are red, berries are blue—be careful how you pick them, or you'll be blue, too!

1 cup oat flour
1 cup all-purpose flour
1-1/2 tablespoons baking powder
1/2 teaspoon baking soda
1/4 cup sugar
1-1/2 cups buttermilk
1/2 cup dairy sour cream
2 eggs
2 tablespoons butter, melted, cooled
3/4 cup blueberries, fresh or frozen, thawed, drained

Vegetable shortening or oil for grids
1 cup butter, melted
Powdered sugar

BLUEBERRY SAUCE:

2 cups blueberries, fresh or frozen, thawed, drained
1/4 cup sugar
2 tablespoons lemon juice
1 teaspoon cornstarch

Preheat waffle iron. Preheat oven to 250°F (120°C). In a medium-size bowl sift together oat flour, all-purpose flour, baking powder, baking soda and sugar. In a large bowl beat together buttermilk, sour cream, eggs and the 2 tablespoons butter. Gradually stir in flour mixture. Beat until smooth. Gently fold blueberries into the batter. Lightly brush hot grids with shortening or oil. Pour enough batter to fill two-thirds of the waffle iron. Cook until crisp and golden-brown. While the waffles are cooking, prepare the Blueberry Sauce. Keep finished waffles warm in the oven on a rack until ready to serve. Repeat with the remaining batter. Serve waffles with melted butter and hot Blueberry Sauce. Sift powdered sugar over the waffles. Serve immediately. Makes about 4 waffles or 4 servings.

BLUEBERRY SAUCE

In a small saucepan over low heat combine blueberries, sugar, lemon juice and cornstarch. Cook, stirring, until cornstarch is dissolved. Cook, stirring, until small bubbles start to appear. Simmer until blueberries start to break apart, about 5 minutes, stirring occasionally. Keep warm until ready to serve. Makes about 1-1/2 cups.

Oatmeal Waffles with Strawberry Syrup

This hearty and delicious waffle is a perfect alternative to a boring bowl of oatmeal. A nice warm treat on a cold winter morning. Kids of all ages will love it.

2 cups water
1 cup old-fashioned rolled oats
1 cup all-purpose flour
3/4 cups oat flour
1-1/2 tablespoons baking powder
1/4 teaspoon baking soda
1/4 teaspoon salt
2 eggs
1/3 cup plain low-fat yogurt
3/4 cup milk

1/2 cup packed dark brown sugar
1/4 cup butter, melted, cooled
Vegetable shortening or oil for grids
1 cup butter, melted

STRAWBERRY SYRUP:

2 cups strawberry preserves
1/2 cup water
3 tablespoons light corn syrup

In a medium-size saucepan bring water to a boil. Stir in 3/4 cup oats. Reduce heat and simmer until all the water is absorbed 4 to 5 minutes. Set aside. Preheat waffle iron. Preheat oven to 250°F (120°C). In a medium-size bowl sift together all-purpose flour, oat flour, baking powder, baking soda and salt. In a large bowl beat together eggs, yogurt, milk, brown sugar and the 1/4 cup butter. Gradually stir in flour mixture. Beat until smooth. Stir in cooked oats. Lightly brush hot grids with shortening or oil. Pour enough batter to fill two-thirds of the waffle iron. Push batter to the edges with a wooden spoon. Sprinkle the top of the batter with 1 tablespoon of the remaining uncooked oats. Batter will be thick. Cook until crisp and golden-brown. While the waffles are cooking, prepare Strawberry Syrup. Keep finished waffles warm in the oven on a rack until ready to serve. Repeat with the remaining batter. Serve waffles with melted butter and hot Strawberry Syrup. Makes about 4 waffles or 4 servings.

STRAWBERRY SYRUP

In a small saucepan combine strawberry preserves, water and light corn syrup over low heat. Cook, stirring, until small bubbles appear around the edges. Simmer 2 to 3 minutes, stirring occasionally. Reduce the heat and keep warm until ready to serve. Makes about 2 cups.

Banana Nut Waffles with Whipped Banana Topping

When the bananas are combined with almonds and walnuts, the flavor is so good that it's rumored even monkeys will go nuts for these waffles!

1 cup all-purpose flour
1 cup oat flour
1-1/2 tablespoons baking powder
1/4 teaspoon baking soda
1/4 teaspoon salt
1/2 cup sugar
3 ripe bananas
2 eggs
1-1/2 teaspoons banana extract
1/2 teaspoon vanilla extract
3/4 cup buttermilk

1/4 cup vegetable oil
1/4 cup slivered almonds
1/4 cup chopped walnuts
Vegetable shortening or oil for grids

WHIPPED BANANA TOPPING:

4 ripe bananas, sliced
1 teaspoon lemon juice
1 cup whipping cream
2 tablespoons sugar

Preheat waffle iron. Preheat oven to 250°F (120°C). In a large bowl sift together all-purpose flour, oat flour, baking powder, baking soda, salt and sugar. In a blender or food processor fitted with the metal blade combine bananas, eggs, banana extract, vanilla, buttermilk and oil. Process until smooth. Gradually stir banana mixture into flour mixture. Beat until smooth. Stir in almonds and walnuts. Lightly brush hot grids with shortening or oil. Pour enough batter to fill two-thirds of the waffle iron. Cook until crisp and golden-brown. While the waffles are cooking, prepare the Whipped Banana Topping. Keep finished waffles warm in the oven on a rack until ready to serve. Repeat with the remaining batter. Serve waffles with Whipped Banana Topping. Makes about 4 waffles or 4 servings.

WHIPPED BANANA TOPPING

In a blender or food processor fitted with the metal blade process banana slices and lemon juice until smooth. In a medium-size bowl whip together cream and sugar, until soft peaks are formed. Fold in banana puree. Keep refrigerated until ready to serve. Makes about 2 cups.

Popi's Buttermilk Waffles

One of my fondest childhood memories is of waking up on Sunday morning with the bright sun shining through my window and the smell of my dad's fresh waffles cooking. Start creating some great family memories of your own with this old-fashioned favorite!

2 cups all-purpose flour
2 teaspoons baking powder
1 teaspoon baking soda
1/4 teaspoon salt
1/4 cup sugar
2 eggs, separated

2 cups buttermilk
3 tablespoons butter, melted, cooled
1 teaspoon vanilla extract
Vegetable shortening or oil for grids
1/2 cup butter, melted
1-1/2 cups maple syrup, warmed

Preheat waffle iron. Preheat oven to 250°F (120°C). In a medium-size bowl sift together flour, baking powder, baking soda, salt and sugar. In a large bowl beat together egg yolks, buttermilk, the 3 tablespoons butter and vanilla. Gradually stir in flour mixture. Beat until smooth. In a small bowl whip egg whites until soft peaks are formed. Fold into batter. Lightly brush hot grids with shortening or oil. Pour enough batter to fill two-thirds of the waffle iron. Cook until crisp and golden-brown. Serve waffles hot with melted butter and warmed maple syrup. Makes about 4 waffles or 4 servings.

Variations: Add 1/4 cup of pecan pieces to the batter before cooking. And for a touch of the blarney, add 4 drops of green food coloring on St. Patrick's Day.

Cinnamon-Raisin Waffles

This traditional bread recipe becomes a wonderful waffle treat that everyone will love. With just enough sweetness and spice, it's the raisins that make this waffle exceptionally nice.

3 tablespoons sugar
1/2 teaspoon ground cinnamon
2 cups all-purpose flour
1-1/2 tablespoons baking powder
1/2 teaspoon baking soda
1/2 cup sugar
1 teaspoon ground cinnamon
2 eggs
1-3/4 cups buttermilk

1/4 cup butter, melted, cooled
2 tablespoons maple syrup
1 teaspoon vanilla extract
1/2 teaspoon orange extract
1/2 cup golden raisins
Vegetable shortening or oil for grids
1 cup butter, melted
1 cup maple syrup, warmed

Preheat waffle iron. Preheat oven to 250°F (120°C). In a small bowl combine the 3 tablespoons sugar and the 1/2 teaspoon cinnamon; set aside. In a medium-size bowl sift together all-purpose flour, baking powder, baking soda, the 1/2 cup sugar and the 1 teaspoon cinnamon. In a large bowl beat together eggs, buttermilk, the 1/4 butter, maple syrup, vanilla and orange extract. Gradually stir in flour mixture. Beat until smooth. Stir in raisins. Lightly brush hot grids with shortening or oil. Pour enough batter to fill two-thirds of the waffle iron. Cook until crisp and golden-brown. Set aside. Keep finished waffles warm in the oven on a rack until ready to serve. Repeat with remaining batter. Serve waffles hot with melted butter and warmed syrup. Sprinkle sugar and cinnamon mixture over the waffles. Makes about 4 waffles or 4 servings.

Strawberry Waffles

This is the perfect answer to "What can we have that's different for brunch?" These waffles taste so much like strawberries, everyone will think you have been out all morning picking them right off the vine.

1 cup all-purpose flour
1 cup oat flour
1/2 cup granulated sugar
2 tablespoons baking powder
1 teaspoon baking soda
1/2 cup strawberry-flavored low-fat yogurt
2 eggs, separated
1/3 cup vegetable oil
2 tablespoons strawberry extract

1 teaspoon vanilla extract
1/2 teaspoon orange extract
1/2 cup strawberry preserves
3 cups coarsely chopped strawberries, fresh or
    frozen, thawed, drained
1/8 teaspoon cream of tartar
Vegetable shortening or oil for grids
Powdered sugar

Preheat waffle iron. Preheat oven to 250°F (120°C). In a medium-size bowl sift together all-purpose flour, oat flour, sugar, baking powder and baking soda. In a large bowl beat together yogurt, egg yolks, oil, strawberry extract, vanilla, orange extract and strawberry preserves. Gradually stir in flour mixture. Beat until smooth. Stir in 1 cup of the strawberries. In a small bowl whip egg whites with cream of tartar until soft peaks are formed. Fold into batter. Lightly brush hot grids with shortening or oil. Pour enough batter to fill two-thirds of the waffle iron. Cook until crisp and light brown. Keep finished waffles warm in the oven on a rack until ready to serve. To serve, place about 1/2 cup of the remaining chopped strawberries on top of each waffle and sift powdered sugar over waffles. Makes about 4 waffles or 4 servings.

Granola Waffles with Blackberry Syrup

These light and crunchy waffles are ideal for a nice, hot breakfast and they're quick and easy to prepare. Plus without the syrup these waffles make great snacks.

1 cup whole-wheat flour
1 tablespoon baking powder
1/2 teaspoon baking soda
2 eggs
3/4 cup plain low-fat yogurt
1-1/2 cups buttermilk
1/4 cup honey
1 teaspoon dark molasses
1/2 cup packed dark brown sugar

1/4 cup butter, melted, cooled
1 cup plain unsweetened granola
Vegetable shortening or oil for grids
1 cup butter, melted

BLACKBERRY SYRUP:

1 teaspoon cornstarch
1/4 cup water
1-1/2 cups blackberry preserves

Preheat waffle iron. Preheat oven to 250°F (120°C). In a medium-size bowl sift together flour, baking powder and baking soda. In a large bowl beat together eggs, yogurt, buttermilk, honey, molasses, brown sugar and the 1/4 cup butter. Gradually stir in flour mixture. Beat until smooth. Stir in granola. Lightly brush hot grids with shortening or oil. Pour enough batter to fill two-thirds of the waffle iron. Cook until crisp and golden-brown. While the waffles are cooking, prepare the Blackberry Syrup. Keep finished waffles warm in the oven on a rack until ready to serve. Repeat with the remaining batter. Serves waffles with melted butter and hot Blackberry Syrup. Makes about 4 waffles or 4 servings.

BLACKBERRY SYRUP

In a small bowl combine cornstarch and water. In a small saucepan combine blackberry preserves and cornstarch mixture over low heat. Cook, stirring, until small bubbles appear around the edges. Keep warm until ready to serve. Makes about 1-1/2 cups.

Ricotta-Cheese Waffles with Raspberry Syrup

This wonderful Italian cheese has been reserved for special pasta dishes. But now the secret is out! Its unassuming cheesy flavor is perfectly blended with this tangy sauce for a delicious breakfast.

1-3/4 cups all-purpose flour
1-1/2 tablespoons baking powder
1/2 teaspoon baking soda
1 teaspoon salt
1 tablespoon granulated sugar
1 cup milk
2 eggs
2 tablespoons vegetable oil

1 cup ricotta cheese
Vegetable shortening or oil for grids
Powdered sugar

RASPBERRY SYRUP:

1-1/2 cups raspberry preserves
1/4 cup hot water
3 tablespoons light corn syrup

Preheat waffle iron. Preheat oven to 250°F (120°C). In a medium-size bowl sift together flour, baking powder, baking soda, salt and granulated sugar. In a large bowl beat together milk, eggs, oil and ricotta cheese. Gradually stir in flour mixture. Beat until smooth. Lightly brush hot grids with shortening or oil. Pour enough batter to fill two-thirds of the waffle iron. Cook until crisp and golden-brown. While the waffles are cooking, prepare the Raspberry Syrup. Keep finished waffles warm in the oven on a rack. Repeat with the remaining batter. Serve waffles with hot Raspberry Syrup and sift powdered sugar over waffles. Makes about 4 waffles or 4 servings.

RASPBERRY SYRUP

In a small saucepan combine raspberry preserves, water and light corn syrup. Slowly warm over low heat until small bubbles appear around the edges. Simmer 2 to 3 minutes. Stir occasionally. Keep warm until ready to serve. Makes about 1-1/2 cups.

Hash Brown Potato Waffles

This is a variation on an old-time country favorite for breakfast with eggs and bacon. They're also good as a hot appetizer or a dinner side dish. In other words, these waffles are good morning, noon and night. Because the the waffles do not fill the sections, they have pretty, lacy edges.

3/4 cup all-purpose flour
1 teaspoon salt
1/2 teaspoon pepper
3 eggs
1 cup buttermilk

1/4 cup vegetable oil
2 medium-size russet potatoes
Vegetable shortening or oil for grids
1 cup dairy sour cream
1 cup applesauce

Preheat waffle iron. Preheat oven to 250°F (120°C). In a medium-size bowl combine flour, salt and pepper. In a large bowl beat together eggs, buttermilk and oil. Gradually stir in flour mixture. Beat until smooth. Grate potatoes with skins. Stir into batter. Lightly brush hot grids with shortening or oil. With a ladle, spoon enough batter to cover one-half of each section of the waffle iron. Close the lid. Cook until crisp and golden-brown. Remove finished waffles with a fork. Keep warm in the oven on a rack until ready to serve. Serve hot waffles with a dab of sour cream and applesauce on top. Makes about 12 sections or 4 servings.

Carob Waffles with Strawberry Sauce

I always thought carob was just something you had to eat while camping in the wilderness, but not anymore. The sweet and nutty taste of carob is perfectly blended in these waffles to satisfy any sweet tooth.

1 cup all-purpose flour
1 cup oat flour
1 tablespoon baking powder
1/4 teaspoon baking soda
2 eggs
3/4 cup plain low-fat yogurt
1 cup milk
2 tablespoons honey
2 tablespoons butter, melted, cooled

3/4 cup carob chips
Vegetable shortening or oil for grids
1 cup butter, melted

STRAWBERRY SAUCE:

2 cups sliced fresh strawberries or 2 cups frozen
   strawberries, thawed, drained
1/2 cup packed light brown sugar
1 tablespoon hot water

Preheat waffle iron. Preheat oven to 250°F (120°C). In a medium-size bowl sift together all-purpose flour, oat flour, baking powder and baking soda. In a large bowl beat together eggs, yogurt, milk, honey and the 2 tablespoons butter. Gradually stir in flour mixture. Beat until smooth. Stir in carob chips. Lightly brush hot grids with shortening or oil. Pour enough batter to fill two-thirds of the waffle iron. Cook until crisp and golden-brown. While the waffles are cooking, prepare the Strawberry Sauce. Keep finished waffles warm in the oven on a rack until ready to serve. Repeat with the remaining batter. Serve waffles with melted butter and hot Strawberry Sauce. Makes about 4 waffles or 4 servings.

STRAWBERRY SAUCE

In a medium-size saucepan combine strawberries, brown sugar and water over medium-low heat. Cook, stirring, until small bubbles start to appear around the edges. Reduce heat and simmer 5 minutes. Keep warm until ready to serve. Makes about 1-1/2 cups.

Cream-Cheese Waffles

These crisp and light waffles have just the right amount of cream cheese flavor. Try them plain or with fresh fruit and you'll be pleasantly surprised. And you thought cream cheese was only good on bagels!

1-1/2 cups all-purpose flour
1 tablespoon baking powder
1/2 teaspoon baking soda
1/2 teaspoon salt
2 eggs

1 cup buttermilk
1/2 cup (4 ounces) cream cheese, softened
1/2 cup dairy sour cream
3 tablespoons vegetable oil
Vegetable shortening or oil for grids

Preheat waffle iron. Preheat oven to 250°F (120°C). In a medium-size bowl sift together flour, baking powder, baking soda and salt. In a large bowl beat together eggs, buttermilk, cream cheese, sour cream and oil. Gradually stir in flour mixture. Beat until smooth. Lightly brush hot grids with shortening or oil. Pour enough batter to fill two-thirds of the waffle iron. Cook until crisp and golden-brown. Keep finished waffles warm in the oven on a rack until ready to serve. Repeat with the remaining batter. Makes about 4 waffles or 4 servings.

Pumpkin Waffles with Cranberry Syrup

Even though pumpkins seem to appear miraculously in the fall, their delightful taste can be enjoyed all year round.

1 cup whole-wheat pastry flour
1 cup all-purpose flour
1 tablespoon baking powder
1/2 teaspoon ground cinnamon
1/4 teaspoon ground cloves
1/2 teaspoon ground nutmeg
1/4 teaspoon salt
2 eggs, separated
1-1/2 cups buttermilk
1/2 cup dairy sour cream

1/4 cup packed light brown sugar
2 tablespoons vegetable oil
3/4 cup canned pumpkin puree
1/2 cup chopped pecans
Vegetable shortening or oil for grid
1 cup butter, melted

CRANBERRY SYRUP:

1 (16-oz.) can jellied cranberry sauce
3/4 cup water
3 tablespoons light corn syrup

Preheat waffle iron. Preheat oven to 250°F (120°C). In a medium-size bowl sift together whole-wheat pastry flour, all-purpose flour, baking powder, cinnamon, cloves, nutmeg and salt. In a large bowl beat together egg yolks, buttermilk, sour cream, brown sugar, oil and pumpkin puree. Gradually stir in flour mixture. Stir in pecans. Beat until blended. In a small bowl whip egg whites until soft peaks are formed. Fold into batter. Batter will be thick. Lightly brush hot grids with shortening or oil. Pour enough batter to fill two-thirds of the waffle iron. Push batter to the edges with a wooden spoon. Cook until crisp and golden-brown. While the waffles are cooking, prepare the Cranberry Syrup. Keep finished waffles warm in the oven on a rack until ready to serve. Repeat with the remaining batter. Serve waffles with melted butter and hot Cranberry Syrup. Makes about 4 waffles or 4 servings.

CRANBERRY SYRUP

In a small saucepan combine cranberry sauce, water and light corn syrup over low heat. Cook, stirring, until small bubbles appear around the edges. Keep warm until ready to serve. Makes about 2 cups.

Avocado Waffles with Apricot Syrup

It's refreshing to think of avocados in different ways other than as a garnish for Mexican food. This beautiful, light green waffle with the zesty Apricot Syrup is unlike anything you've ever tasted.

1 avocado, cut into 1-inch pieces
1 tablespoon lemon juice
1/4 cup cream cheese, softened
1-1/4 cups buttermilk
2 eggs
2 tablespoons vegetable oil
1-1/4 cups all-purpose flour
1/2 cup oat flour
1 tablespoon baking powder
1/2 teaspoon baking soda

1/2 teaspoon salt
1/4 cup granulated sugar
Vegetable shortening or oil for grids
Powdered sugar

APRICOT SYRUP:

2 cups apricot preserves
1/2 cup orange juice
3 tablespoons light corn syrup
1 teaspoon sugar

Preheat waffle iron. Preheat oven to 250°F (120°C). In a blender or food processor fitted with the metal blade combine avocado, lemon juice, cream cheese, buttermilk, eggs and oil. Process until smooth. In a large bowl sift together all-purpose flour, oat flour, baking powder, baking soda, salt and granulated sugar. Gradually stir in avocado mixture. Beat until smooth. Lightly brush hot grids with shortening or oil. Pour enough batter to fill two-thirds of the waffle iron. Cook until crisp and golden-brown. While waffles are cooking, prepare the Apricot Syrup. Keep finished waffles warm in the oven on a rack until ready to serve. Repeat with the remaining batter. Serve waffles with hot Apricot Syrup. Sift powdered sugar over the waffles. Makes about 4 waffles or 4 servings.

APRICOT SYRUP

In a small saucepan combine apricot preserves, orange juice, light corn syrup and sugar over low heat. Cook, stirring, until small bubbles appear around the edges. Stir occasionally. Simmer 2 to 3 minutes. Keep warm until ready to serve. Makes about 2 cups.

Almond-Butter Waffles with Raspberries

These waffles possess a wonderfully unique nutty flavor that seems to come to life with the tart taste of the raspberries. Because they stay so moist and fresh they make a great snack any time of the day. Almond butter is available at natural food stores and gourmet markets.

1-1/4 cups all-purpose flour
3/4 cup oat flour
1 tablespoon baking powder
1/4 teaspoon baking soda
1/4 teaspoon salt
2 eggs
2 cups buttermilk

1/4 cup butter, melted, cooled
1/4 cup packed light brown sugar
1/3 cup almond butter
Vegetable shortening or oil for grids
2 cups raspberries
Powdered sugar

Preheat waffle iron. Preheat oven to 250°F (120°C). In a medium-size bowl sift together all-purpose flour, oat flour, baking powder, baking soda and salt. In a large bowl beat together eggs, buttermilk, butter, brown sugar and almond butter. Gradually stir in flour mixture. Beat until smooth. Lightly brush hot grids with shortening or oil. Pour enough batter to fill two-thirds of the waffle iron. Cook until crisp and golden-brown. Keep finished waffles warm in the oven on a rack until ready to serve. Repeat with the remaining batter. Serve waffles hot with fresh raspberries. Sift powdered sugar over the waffles. Makes about 4 waffles or 4 servings.

Variations:
Cashew-Butter Waffles: Replace almond butter with 1/3 cup cashew butter.
Peanut-Butter Waffles: Replace almond butter with 1/3 cup smooth peanut butter.

Bran Muffin Waffles with Apricot Syrup

These nutritious waffles are delicious and surprisingly light. And with the Apricot Sauce they're a lot more fun than a muffin!

1 cup all-purpose flour
3/4 cup oat flour
1 tablespoon baking powder
1/2 teaspoon baking soda
1/4 teaspoon salt
2 eggs
1-3/4 cups buttermilk

2 tablespoons vegetable oil
1/4 cup packed dark brown sugar
1 cup unprocessed wheat bran
Vegetable shortening or oil for grids
1 cup butter, melted
Apricot Syrup (page 38)

Preheat waffle iron. Preheat oven to 250°F (120°C). In a medium-size bowl sift together all-purpose flour, oat flour, baking powder, baking soda and salt. In a large bowl beat together eggs, buttermilk, oil and brown sugar. Gradually stir in flour mixture. Beat until smooth. Stir in bran. Lightly brush hot grids with shortening or oil. Pour enough batter to fill two-thirds of the waffle iron. Cook until crisp and golden-brown. While the waffles are cooking, prepare the Apricot Syrup. Keep finished waffles warm in the oven on a rack until ready to serve. Repeat with the remaining batter. Serve waffles with melted butter and hot Apricot Syrup. Makes about 4 waffles or 4 servings.

Cantaloupe Waffles with Papaya Custard Sauce

We used to call cantaloupe the wedding fruit because if you eat them you can't elope! Married or single everyone is bound to love this pretty orange treat.

2 cups all-purpose flour
1-1/2 tablespoons baking powder
1/2 teaspoon baking soda
1/4 teaspoon salt
1/3 cup sugar
1 cantaloupe, cut into 2-inch pieces
2 eggs
2 tablespoons vegetable oil
1/4 cup plain low-fat yogurt

Vegetable shortening or oil for grids
1 cup fresh blueberries

PAPAYA CUSTARD SAUCE:

1 papaya
1/2 cup whipping cream
3/4 cup milk
3 tablespoons sugar
3 egg yolks
2 tablespoons peach preserves

Prepare Papaya Custard Sauce. Preheat waffle iron. Preheat oven to 250°F (120°C). In a medium-size bowl sift together flour, baking powder, baking soda, salt and sugar. In a blender or food processor fitted with the metal blade process cantaloupe pieces until smooth. Transfer to a large bowl; add eggs, oil and yogurt. Beat until combined. Gradually stir in flour mixture. Beat until smooth. Lightly brush hot grids with shortening or oil. Pour enough batter to fill two-thirds of the waffle iron. Cook until crisp and golden-brown. Keep finished waffles warm in the oven on a rack until ready to serve. Repeat with the remaining batter. Serve waffles with hot Papaya Custard Sauce. Top with blueberries. Makes about 4 waffles or 4 servings.

PAPAYA CUSTARD SAUCE

Cut papaya in half, remove seeds and cut into 2-inch pieces. In a blender or food processor fitted with the metal blade process papaya pieces until smooth. Press through a fine sieve. Set aside. In a medium-size saucepan combine cream, milk and sugar. Cook over low heat, stirring, until small bubbles appear around the edges. In a small bowl whisk egg yolks until light. Add to hot mixture. Simmer until thickened, 10 to 15 minutes. Stir occasionally. Keep warm over warm water until ready to serve. Just before serving, stir in papaya puree and peach preserves. Makes about 1-1/2 cups.

Raspberry Waffles with Creamy Raspberry Sauce

The only thing better than eating fresh raspberries right off the vine is eating a hot raspberry waffle right off the waffle maker.

1-1/2 cups all-purpose flour
1/2 cup oat flour
1 tablespoon baking powder
1/2 teaspoon baking soda
1/4 cup sugar
2 eggs
1-1/2 cups half and half
1/2 teaspoon vanilla extract
1/4 cup vegetable oil

1 cup raspberries, fresh or frozen, thawed,
    drained
Vegetable shortening or oil for grids

CREAMY RASPBERRY SAUCE:

2 cups whipping cream
1/4 cup sugar
1/4 cup raspberry preserves
1 cup fresh raspberries

Preheat waffle iron. Preheat oven to 250°F (120°C). In a medium-size bowl sift together all-purpose flour, oat flour, baking powder, baking soda and sugar. In a large bowl beat together eggs, half and half, vanilla and oil. Gradually stir in flour mixture. Beat until smooth. Gently fold in raspberries. Lightly brush hot grids with shortening or oil. Pour enough batter to fill two-thirds of the waffle iron. Cook until crisp and golden-brown. While the waffles are cooking, prepare Creamy Raspberry Sauce. Keep finished waffles warm in the oven on a rack until ready to serve. Repeat with the remaining batter. Serve waffles with hot Creamy Raspberry Sauce. Makes about 4 waffles or 4 servings.

CREAMY RASPBERRY SAUCE

In a medium-size saucepan combine cream and sugar over medium-low heat. Cook, stirring, until small bubbles start to appear around the edges. Reduce heat and stir in raspberry preserves. Simmer 2 minutes. Remove from heat and let stand 3 to 5 minutes. Sauce will thicken. Gently fold in raspberries. Stir until coated. Makes about 2-1/2 cups.

Hawaiian Waffles with Tropical Fruit

These waffles are a cumulation of all sorts of delicious Hawaiian tastes. They're so good that if you close your eyes, within moments you can feel the cool, enchanting Pacific breezes. Aloha!

2 cups all-purpose flour
1 tablespoon baking powder
2 eggs, separated
3/4 cup pineapple-coconut nectar
1/2 cup papaya nectar
1/2 cup sweetened condensed milk
3 tablespoons fresh lime juice
1/2 cup packed light brown sugar
1/4 cup vegetable oil
1/2 cup crushed pineapple, fresh or canned, drained

1 cup macadamia nuts, halved
1/2 cup flaked coconut
Vegetable shortening or oil for grids

TROPICAL FRUIT TOPPING:

2 papayas, cut into 1-inch pieces
4 kiwifruit, sliced
2 cups sliced strawberries
2 cups pineapple chunks, fresh or canned, drained
1/2 cup flaked coconut

Preheat waffle iron. Preheat oven to 250°F (120°C). In a medium-size bowl sift together flour and baking powder. In a large bowl beat together egg yolks, pineapple-coconut nectar, papaya nectar, condensed milk, lime juice, brown sugar and oil. Gradually stir in flour mixture. Beat until smooth. Stir in pineapple, macadamia nuts and coconut. In a small bowl whip egg whites until soft peaks are formed. Fold into batter. Lightly brush hot grids with shortening or oil. Pour enough batter to fill two-thirds of the waffle iron. Cook until crisp and golden-brown. While the waffles are cooking, prepare the Tropical Fruit Topping. Keep finished waffles warm in the oven on a rack until ready to serve. Repeat with the remaining batter. Serve waffles hot with a spoonful of fruit. Sprinkle a few tablespoons of the reserved coconut over the topping. Makes about 4 waffles or 4 servings.

TROPICAL FRUIT TOPPING

In a large bowl combine papaya pieces, kiwifruit slices, strawberry slices and pineapple chunks. Keep refrigerated until ready to serve. Reserve coconut for sprinkling. Makes about 5 cups.

Apricot-Pecan Waffles with Pineapple-Apricot Sauce

This tart and nutty morning eye-opener is a wholesome way to get your family's morning started off on the right foot. This sweet sauce appeals to everyone's taste buds.

1 cup all-purpose flour
1 cup oat flour
1-1/2 tablespoons baking powder
1/2 teaspoon baking soda
2 eggs, separated
2 cups buttermilk
3/4 cup packed dark brown sugar
1/3 cup butter, melted, cooled
1/2 cup chopped pecans

1/2 cup dried apricots, cut into quarters
Vegetable shortening or oil for grids
Powdered sugar

PINEAPPLE-APRICOT SAUCE:

1 cup fresh or canned pineapple chunks, drained
3/4 cup apricot preserves
1/4 cup hot water

Preheat waffle iron. Preheat oven to 250°F (120°C). In a medium-size bowl sift together all-purpose flour, oat flour, baking powder and baking soda. In a large bowl beat together egg yolks, buttermilk, brown sugar and butter. Gradually stir in flour mixture. Beat until smooth. Stir in pecans and dried apricot pieces. In a small bowl whip egg whites until soft peaks are formed. Fold into batter. Lightly brush hot grids with shortening or oil. Pour enough batter to fill two-thirds of the waffle iron. Push batter to the edges with a wooden spoon. Cook until crisp and golden-brown. While the waffles are cooking, prepare the Pineapple-Apricot Sauce. Keep finished waffles warm in the oven on a rack until ready to serve. Repeat with the remaining batter. Serve waffles with hot Pineapple-Apricot Sauce. Sift powdered sugar over the top. Serve immediately. Makes about 4 waffles or 4 servings.

PINEAPPLE-APRICOT SAUCE

In a small saucepan heat pineapple chunks, apricot preserves and water over low heat, stirring occasionally. Do not boil. Keep warm until ready to serve. Makes about 2 cups.

Lemon-Yogurt Waffles with Honey-Pear Topping

Light and tangy these lemony waffles offer a wonderful, healthful antidote to the Monday morning blues, especially when served with this zesty Honey-Pear Topping—and besides everyone knows that "pears" love honey!

2 cups all-purpose flour
1 tablespoon baking powder
1/2 teaspoon baking soda
2 tablespoons sugar
2 eggs, separated
1 cup lemon-flavored low-fat yogurt
3/4 cup milk
2 teaspoons lemon extract
2 tablespoons vegetable oil
Vegetable shortening or oil for grids

1-1/2 cups plain low-fat yogurt
1 lemon, thinly sliced for garnish

HONEY-PEAR TOPPING:

4 Anjou pears, peeled, cored, cut into bite-size
 pieces
1/3 cup clover honey
1 cup plain granola
1 teaspoon grated orange zest

Preheat waffle iron. Preheat oven to 250°F (120°C). In a medium-size bowl sift together flour, baking powder, baking soda and sugar. In a large bowl beat together egg yolks, yogurt, milk, lemon extract and oil. Gradually stir in flour mixture. Beat until smooth. In a small bowl whip egg whites until soft peaks are formed. Fold into batter. Lightly brush hot grids with shortening or oil. Pour enough batter to fill two-thirds of the waffle iron. Cook until crisp and golden-brown. While the waffles are cooking, prepare the Honey-Pear Topping. Keep finished waffles warm in the oven on a rack until ready to serve. Repeat with the remaining batter. Serve waffles with plain yogurt and Honey-Pear Topping. Garnish with lemon slices. Makes about 4 waffles or 4 servings.

HONEY-PEAR TOPPING

In a medium-size bowl combine pear pieces, honey, granola and orange zest. Stir until pears are coated and all ingredients are combined. Set aside until ready to serve. Makes about 2 cups.

Yam 'n' Banana Waffles with Maple Syrup

These waffles are as much fun to say as they are to eat! Rich in texture and flavor they have the "right stuff" to get you through a hectic morning!

3 bananas, peeled
1 (16-oz.) can cut yams in light syrup
1/2 teaspoon vanilla extract
2 eggs
1/2 cup milk
1/4 cup vegetable oil
1-3/4 cups oat flour

1 tablespoon baking powder
1/4 teaspoon baking soda
1 teaspoon ground nutmeg
1/2 cup chopped pecans
Vegetable shortening or oil for grids
1 cup butter, melted
1 cup maple syrup, warmed

Preheat waffle iron. Preheat oven to 250°F (120°C). In a blender or food processor fitted with the metal blade combine bananas and yams with syrup. Process until smooth. Add vanilla, eggs, milk and oil. Continue to process until all ingredients are blended thoroughly. Transfer to a large bowl. In a medium-size bowl sift together oat flour, baking powder, baking soda and nutmeg. Gradually stir into banana mixture. Beat until smooth. Stir in pecans. Lightly brush hot grids with shortening or oil. Pour enough batter to fill two-thirds of the waffle iron. Cook until crisp and golden-brown. Keep finished waffles warm in the oven on a rack until ready to serve. Repeat with the remaining batter. Serve waffles with melted butter and warm maple syrup. Makes about 4 waffles or 4 servings.

Cranberry Waffles with Orange-Apricot Syrup

This waffle is a warm and wonderful holiday treat. What better way to enjoy your Thanksgiving weekend than with a festive brunch. Discover your own family's traditions.

2-1/4 cups all-purpose flour
1-1/2 tablespoons baking powder
1/4 teaspoon baking soda
1/2 cup granulated sugar
1/4 teaspoon salt
2 eggs
1/2 cup orange juice
1-1/4 cups buttermilk
1/4 teaspoon vanilla extract
1/3 cup vegetable oil

1 tablespoon grated orange zest
1 cup fresh cranberries
1/2 cup chopped walnuts
Vegetable shortening or oil for grids
Powdered sugar

ORANGE-APRICOT SYRUP:

1-1/2 cups apricot preserves
3 tablespoons orange marmalade
3 tablespoons orange juice
3 tablespoons light corn syrup

Preheat waffle iron. Preheat oven to 250°F (120°C). In a medium-size bowl sift together flour, baking powder, baking soda, granulated sugar and salt. In a large bowl beat together eggs, orange juice, buttermilk, vanilla, oil and orange zest. Gradually stir in flour mixture. Beat until smooth. Fold cranberries and walnuts into batter. Lightly brush hot grids with shortening or oil. Pour enough batter to fill two-thirds of the waffle iron. Cook until crisp and golden-brown. While the waffles are cooking prepare the Orange-Apricot Syrup. Keep finished waffles warm in the oven on a rack until ready to serve. Repeat with the remaining batter. Serve waffles with hot Orange-Apricot Syrup. Sift powdered sugar over the waffles. Serve immediately. Makes about 4 waffles or 4 servings.

ORANGE-APRICOT SYRUP

In a small saucepan combine apricot preserves, orange marmalade, orange juice and light corn syrup over low heat. Cook, stirring, until small bubbles appear around the edges. Simmer 2 to 3 minutes. Keep warm until ready to serve. Makes about 1-1/2 cups.

The Benjie Special—Onion Waffles
with Cream Cheese & Lox

These waffles are perfect for Sunday brunch while reading the newspaper, this twist on an old favorite is sure to delight.

1/4 cup butter
1 medium-size onion, finely chopped
1 cup all-purpose flour
1/2 cup rye flour
1 tablespoon baking powder
1/2 teaspoon baking soda
1 teaspoon salt
2 eggs

1/2 cup dairy sour cream
1-1/4 cups buttermilk
Vegetable shortening or oil for grids
1 (8-oz.) package cream cheese, softened
1 medium-size onion, thinly sliced
8 ounces nova lox or smoked salmon

Preheat waffle iron. Preheat oven to 250°F (120°C). In a medium-size skillet melt butter over medium heat. Add onion and cook until onion starts to turn brown. Remove from heat. Set aside. In a medium-size bowl sift together all-purpose flour, rye flour, baking powder, baking soda and salt. In a large bowl beat together eggs, sour cream and buttermilk. Gradually stir in flour mixture. Beat until smooth. Stir in onion and butter. Lightly brush hot grids with shortening or oil. Ladle enough batter to fill one-half of each section of the waffle iron. (Do not overfill.) Cook until crisp and golden-brown. Keep finished waffles warm in the oven on a rack until ready to serve. Repeat with the remaining batter. To serve spread a layer of cream cheese on each section. Place a onion slice and a nova lox slice on top. Makes about 12 sections or 4 servings.

Belgian Waffles

This yeast batter has been specially designed to be prepared in a Belgian waffle iron. Even though Belgian waffles date back centuries, it wasn't until the 1950s that this European taste was introduced to the world at the World Exposition in Brussels. These crisp waffles are ideal for brunch or dessert. Bon Appetit!

1-1/2 cups milk
1 (1/4-oz.) package fast-rising yeast
2 cups all-purpose flour
1/4 cup sugar
1/2 teaspoon salt
3 eggs, separated

1 teaspoon vanilla extract
1/4 cup butter, melted, cooled
1 teaspoon grated orange zest
Vegetable shortening or oil for grids
1 cup whipping cream
2 cups fresh strawberries, halved

In a small saucepan slowly heat milk until warm to the touch, about 110°F (45°C). Transfer warmed milk to a small bowl. Add yeast and stir to dissolve. Set aside 5 minutes, until frothy. In a medium-size bowl sift together flour, sugar and salt. In a large bowl beat together egg yolks, vanilla and butter. Stir in yeast mixture. Gradually stir in flour mixture. Beat until smooth. Stir in grated orange zest. Cover; let rise in a warm place 2 hours, or until batter has doubled in size. After 2 hours preheat waffle iron. Preheat oven to 250°F (120°C). Lightly brush hot grids with shortening or oil. Pour enough batter to fill two-thirds of the waffle iron. Cook until crisp and light brown. While the waffles are cooking, whip cream until soft peaks are formed. Keep refrigerated until ready to serve. Keep finished waffles warm in the oven on a rack until ready to serve. Serve waffles hot with strawberries and whipped cream on top. Makes about 4 waffles or 4 servings.

Power Waffles with Fresh Berries & Yogurt

These "high-octane" waffles are chock-full of every kind of nutritious ingredient imaginable.

2 cups whole-wheat flour
1 tablespoon baking powder
1/4 teaspoon baking soda
1/2 cup wheat germ
1/2 cup plain low-fat yogurt
1-1/2 cups buttermilk

1/4 cup honey
2 eggs
3 tablespoons vegetable oil
Vegetable shortening or oil for grids
2 cups fresh strawberries, halved
2 cups plain low-fat yogurt

Preheat waffle iron. Preheat oven to 250°F (120°C). In a medium-size bowl sift together flour, baking powder and baking soda. Stir in wheat germ. In a large bowl beat together yogurt, buttermilk, honey, eggs and oil. Gradually stir in flour mixture. Beat until smooth. Batter will be thick. Lightly brush hot grids with shortening or oil. Pour enough batter to fill two-thirds of the waffle iron. Push batter to the edges with a wooden spoon. Cook until crisp and golden-brown. While the waffles are cooking, in a medium-size bowl fold strawberry halves into yogurt. Keep refrigerated until ready to serve. Keep finished waffles warm in the oven on a rack until ready to serve. Repeat with the remaining batter. Serve waffles hot with strawberry and yogurt mixture. Makes about 4 waffles or 4 servings.

Peaches & Cream Waffles

This southern favorite of peaches and cream can now be enjoyed in a hearty and delicious waffle.

1 cup barley flour
1 cup all-purpose flour
1 tablespoon baking powder
1/4 cup sugar
2 eggs, separated
1-1/2 cups milk
1/2 cup whipping cream
1 tablespoon lemon juice
1/4 cup vegetable oil

1 teaspoon vanilla extract
1/4 teaspoon almond extract
1/2 cup peach preserves
Vegetable shortening or oil for grids

PEACHES & CREAM TOPPING

1 cup whipping cream
1 (16-oz.) can peach slices in natural syrup
1/4 cup sugar

Preheat waffle iron. Preheat oven to 250°F (120°C). In a medium-size bowl sift together barley flour, all-purpose flour, baking powder and sugar. In a large bowl beat together egg yolks, milk, cream, lemon juice, oil, vanilla and almond extract. Gradually stir in flour mixture. Beat until smooth. Stir in peach preserves. In a small bowl whip egg whites until soft peaks are formed. Fold into batter. Lightly brush hot grids with shortening or oil. Pour enough batter to fill two-thirds of the waffle iron. Cook until crisp and golden-brown. While the waffles are cooking, prepare the Peaches & Cream Topping. Keep finished waffles warm in the oven on a rack until ready to serve. Repeat with the remaining batter. To serve, place a spoonful of whipped cream on top of each waffle. Place a few hot peach slices on top of whipped cream and spoon hot peach syrup over the top. Makes about 4 waffles or 4 servings.

PEACHES & CREAM TOPPING

In a small bowl whip cream until soft peaks are formed. Keep refrigerated until ready to serve. In a medium-size saucepan slowly warm peach slices with syrup and sugar. Simmer over low heat about 3 minutes. Stir occasionally. Do not boil. Keep warm until ready to serve. Makes about 2 cups.

Mandarin Orange Waffles with Orange-Marmalade Topping

This sweet fruit becomes an exotic delight when it's served for breakfast.

1-1/2 cups all-purpose flour
1/2 cup sugar
1 tablespoon baking powder
1/2 teaspoon baking soda
1 (11-oz.) can mandarin oranges in light syrup
2 eggs, separated
1/2 cup half and half

1/4 cup vegetable oil
Vegetable shortening or oil for grids

ORANGE-MARMALADE TOPPING

1 cup orange marmalade
1/4 cup water
4 egg whites
1 teaspoon cream of tartar

Preheat waffle iron. Preheat oven to 250°F (120°C). In a medium-size bowl sift together flour, sugar, baking powder and baking soda. Drain syrup from oranges into a large bowl. Add egg yolks, half and half and oil. Beat until all ingredients are combined. Gradually stir in flour mixture. Beat until smooth. Carefully stir in orange sections. In a small bowl whip egg whites until soft peaks are formed. Fold into batter. Lightly brush hot grids with shortening or oil. Pour enough batter to fill two-thirds of the waffle iron. Cook until crisp and golden-brown. While the waffles are cooking, prepare the Orange-Marmalade Topping. Keep finished waffles warm in the oven on a rack until ready to serve. Repeat with the remaining batter. Serve waffles hot with Orange-Marmalade Topping. Makes about 4 waffles or 4 servings.

ORANGE-MARMALADE TOPPING

In a small saucepan slowly warm orange marmalade with water over low heat until small bubbles appear around the edges, stirring occasionally. Do not boil. In a medium-size bowl whip egg whites with cream of tartar until soft peaks are formed. Just before serving, carefully fold marmalade syrup into egg whites. Makes about 1-1/2 cups.

LUNCH

These waffles offer the perfect solution to the midday doldrums. They're ideal for luncheons or showers with almost any main-dish salad resting deliciously upon the light and nutritional waffles. Innovative twists give new life to old standbys. Hot, waffles become the perfect accompaniment to soup or a green salad. No matter how you fix them these waffles will brighten up your day.

Egg Salad on Poppy Seed Waffles

Serve these scrumptious waffles piping hot with a scoop of egg salad. These have what it takes to give you enough energy to continue throughout the day.

2 cups all-purpose flour
1 tablespoon baking powder
1/2 teaspoon baking soda
1/4 teaspoon salt
2 tablespoons sugar
2 eggs, separated
2 cups buttermilk
1/4 teaspoon vanilla extract
2 tablespoons vegetable oil
2 tablespoons poppy seeds
Vegetable shortening or oil for grids
6 lettuce leaves
1 tomato, sliced

EGG SALAD:

8 eggs
3 tablespoons diced sweet pickles
3/4 cup diced celery
3 tablespoons chopped green onions
1-1/2 tablespoons Dijon-style mustard
1/4 cup mayonnaise
1/2 teaspoon paprika
1/4 teaspoon salt
1/4 teaspoon pepper

Prepare Egg Salad. Preheat waffle iron. Preheat oven to 250°F (120°C). In a medium-size bowl sift together flour, baking powder, baking soda, salt and sugar. In a large bowl beat together egg yolks, buttermilk, vanilla and oil. Gradually stir in flour mixture. Beat until smooth. Stir in poppy seeds. In a small bowl whip egg whites until soft peaks are formed. Fold into batter. Lightly brush hot grids with shortening or oil. Pour enough batter to fill two-thirds of the waffle iron. Cook until crisp and golden-brown. Keep finished waffles warm in the oven on a rack until ready to serve. Repeat with the remaining batter. To serve, place 1 lettuce leaf on top of each waffle. Place tomato slices and a scoop of Egg Salad on the lettuce. Makes about 4 waffles or 4 servings.

EGG SALAD

Add eggs to a large saucepan; add enough water to cover eggs. Bring water to a boil. Remove from heat, cover and let stand 15 minutes. Remove from saucepan and hold under cold water to peel. Chop eggs. In a large bowl mix together with a fork, eggs, pickles, celery, green onions, mustard, mayonnaise, paprika, salt and pepper. Stir until thoroughly blended. Keep refrigerated until ready to serve. Makes about 3 cups.

Quiche on Whole-Wheat Waffles

Quiche is wonderful because it combines all of the basic food groups in every bite. And what better way to accentuate each of these delicious flavors than to serve it on top of a hot, aromatic whole-wheat waffle?

1 cup whole-wheat flour
3/4 cup all-purpose flour
1 tablespoon baking powder
1/2 teaspoon baking soda
1/2 cup milk
1 cup buttermilk
1/4 cup vegetable oil
2 eggs
1/4 cup packed dark brown sugar
1/4 cup pine nuts
Vegetable shortening or oil for grids

QUICHE:

2 tablespoons olive oil

1 garlic clove, minced
1 cup sliced mushrooms
1 medium-size onion, chopped
8 eggs
1/4 teaspoon salt
1/4 teaspoon ground nutmeg
1/4 teaspoon black pepper
Dash of red (cayenne) pepper
1/4 teaspoon paprika
1 cup shredded Cheddar cheese (4 ounces)
1/4 cup milk
1/4 cup chopped red bell pepper
1/4 cup grated Parmesan cheese (3/4 ounce)

Prepare the Quiche. Preheat waffle iron. In a medium-size bowl sift together whole-wheat flour, all-purpose flour, baking powder and baking soda. In a large bowl beat together milk, buttermilk, oil, eggs and brown sugar. Gradually stir in flour mixture. Beat until smooth. Stir in pine nuts. Lightly brush hot grids with shortening or oil. Pour enough batter to fill two-thirds of the waffle iron. Cook until crisp and golden-brown. Keep finished waffles warm in the oven on a rack until ready to serve. Repeat with the remaining batter. To serve, cut waffles into quarter or half sections and place a slice of Quiche diagonally on each waffle section. Makes about 4 waffles or 6 to 8 servings.

QUICHE

Preheat oven to 350°F (175°C). Grease well a 9-inch casserole dish. In a medium-size skillet heat olive oil. Add garlic, mushrooms and onion and sauté until soft. Set aside. In a medium-size bowl slightly beat eggs. Stir in salt, nutmeg, black pepper, cayenne, paprika, Cheddar cheese, milk, red bell pepper and sautéed mixture. Stir until all ingredients are combined. Pour into prepared casserole dish. Sprinkle Parmesan cheese over the top and bake 30 to 40 minutes or until tester inserted in the center comes out clean. Place Quiche on a rack to cool 10 minutes before serving. Cut Quiche into 6 to 8 slices. Reduce the oven temperature to 250°F (120°C).

Rich Brown-Bread Waffles

These waffles live up to their rich name. Fashioned after the classic bread, they're delicious for lunch with a salad or hot bowl of your favorite soup or all by themselves—indulge yourself!

3/4 cup all-purpose flour
3/4 cup whole-wheat flour
1 tablespoon unsweetened cocoa powder
1-1/2 tablespoons baking powder
1/4 teaspoon baking soda
1-1/2 teaspoons instant espresso coffee
2 eggs, separated
3/4 cup dairy sour cream
1/2 cup buttermilk
1/4 cup dark molasses

1/4 cup vegetable oil
3/4 cup packed dark brown sugar
2 tablespoons dark rum
1/2 teaspoon almond extract
1/2 cup currants
1/2 cup sliced almonds
1/2 cup chopped walnuts
Vegetable shortening or oil for grids
1 (8-oz.) package cream cheese, softened

Preheat waffle iron. Preheat oven to 250°F (120°C). In a medium-size bowl sift together all-purpose flour, whole-wheat flour, cocoa powder, baking powder, baking soda and instant espresso. In a large bowl beat together egg yolks, sour cream, buttermilk, molasses, oil, brown sugar, rum and almond extract. Gradually stir in flour mixture. Beat until smooth. Stir in currants, almonds and walnuts. In a small bowl whip egg whites until soft peaks are formed. Fold into batter. Batter will be thick. Lightly brush hot grids with shortening or oil. Pour enough batter to fill two-thirds of the waffle iron. Push batter to the edges with a wooden spoon. Cook until crisp and a rich brown. Keep finished waffles warm in the oven on a rack until ready to serve. Repeat with the remaining batter. To serve cut waffles into quarter sections. Serve hot with cream cheese on the top. Makes about 3 waffles or 6 servings.

Cheeseburgers on Pumpernickel Waffles

These yeast waffles are superb and hearty enough to satisfy even the most voracious appetites. But don't stop with a cheeseburger because these waffles are equally good with chicken or tuna salad.

1-1/4 cups milk
1 (1/4-oz.) package fast-rising yeast
1 cup all-purpose flour
3/4 cup rye flour
1 teaspoon sugar
1 teaspoon salt
1/2 teaspoon baking soda
1/4 cup dairy sour cream
2 eggs, separated
2 tablespoons dark molasses
2 tablespoons vegetable oil

1-1/2 tablespoons caraway seeds
1/4 cup rolled oats
Vegetable shortening or oil for grids
1-1/2 pounds lean ground beef or ground turkey, shaped into 4 rounds
1/3 cup thousand island dressing
Dijon-style mustard
8 lettuce leaves
1 small red onion, thinly sliced
1 tomato, thinly sliced
1/2 pound Monterey jack cheese, thinly sliced

In a small saucepan slowly heat milk until warm to the touch, about 110°F (45°C). Transfer warmed milk to a small bowl. Add yeast and stir to dissolve. Set aside 5 minutes, until frothy. In a medium-size bowl sift together all-purpose flour, rye flour, sugar, salt and baking soda. In a large bowl beat together sour cream, egg yolks, molasses and oil. Stir in yeast mixture. Gradually stir in flour mixture. Beat until smooth. Stir in caraway seeds. In a small bowl whip egg whites until soft peaks are formed. Fold into batter. Cover; let rise in a warm place 3 hours. After the batter has risen, preheat waffle iron. Preheat oven to 250°F (120°C). Lightly brush hot grids with shortening or oil. Pour enough batter to fill two-thirds of the waffle iron. Sprinkle 1 tablespoon of the oats on top. Cook until crisp and a rich brown. While the waffles are cooking, cook burgers under the broiler or in a large skillet until cooked as desired. Keep finished waffles warm in the oven on a rack until ready to serve. Repeat with remaining batter. To serve, cut waffles into quarter or half sections. Spread a layer of thousand island dressing and mustard on one section. Place lettuce, onion, tomato and cooked beef or turkey burgers on top. Layer cheese slices over burgers. Place under the broiler until cheese is melted. Serve immediately. Makes about 3 waffles or 4 servings.

Spinach & Swiss-Cheese Waffles

Perfect for an all-in-one lunch with a salad on the side—think of these waffles as a square quiche. Prepare ahead of time and just warm in a microwave to have a hot, fresh meal at the office.

1/2 cup butter
1 garlic clove, minced
2 tablespoons chopped green onions
2 tablespoons chopped parsley
1/2 teaspoon sugar
1/4 teaspoon salt
1/2 teaspoon pepper
1/2 teaspoon ground nutmeg
1/2 teaspoon onion powder
1/2 teaspoon chopped fresh oregano
1/2 teaspoon lemon juice
1 pound (1 bunch) spinach, rinsed well, stems removed

1/4 cup sliced mushrooms
3/4 cup rice flour
1 cup all-purpose flour
1-1/2 tablespoons baking powder
1/2 teaspoon baking soda
1/2 cup dairy sour cream
1 cup buttermilk
3 eggs
1/3 cup vegetable oil
2/3 cup shredded Swiss cheese (about 3 ounces)
Vegetable shortening or oil for grids
1 cup butter

Preheat waffle iron. Preheat oven to 250°F (120°C). In a medium-size skillet melt the 1/2 cup butter. Add garlic and lightly brown. Add green onions, parsley, sugar, salt, pepper, nutmeg, onion powder, oregano and lemon juice. Stir constantly 1 minute over medium heat. Stir in spinach and mushrooms. Cover and reduce heat. Cook until spinach is wilted and mushrooms are soft 2 to 3 minutes. Set aside. In a medium-size bowl sift together rice flour, all-purpose flour, baking powder and baking soda. In a large bowl beat together sour cream, buttermilk, eggs and oil. Gradually stir in flour mixture. Beat until smooth. Stir in spinach mixture and Swiss cheese. Batter will be thick. Lightly brush hot grids with shortening or oil. Pour enough batter to fill two-thirds of the waffle iron. Push batter to the edges with a wooden spoon. Cook until crisp and golden-brown. Keep finished waffles warm in the oven on a rack until ready to serve. Serve hot waffles in quarter or half sections with butter. Makes about 4 waffles or 4 servings.

Albacore Melt on Rye Waffles

This is a zesty way to spruce up the age-old tuna melt. Quick and easy to prepare it's the complete mid-day meal with staying power.

1 cup rye flour
1 cup all-purpose flour
1 tablespoon baking powder
1/4 teaspoon baking soda
1 tablespoon salt
2 cups buttermilk
1/4 cup vegetable oil
2 eggs
2 tablespoons vodka
1-1/2 teaspoons dark molasses
1-1/2 tablespoons caraway seeds
Vegetable shortening or oil for grids
2 large tomatoes, sliced

1 cup alfalfa sprouts
1 cup shredded Monterey jack cheese (4 ounces)

ALBACORE TUNA SALAD:

1 (12-1/2-oz.) can albacore tuna in spring water, drained
2 tablespoons mayonnaise
1/4 cup finely chopped onion
1/4 cup finely chopped red bell pepper
1/4 teaspoon salt
1/8 teaspoon pepper
Dash of paprika

Preheat waffle iron. In a medium-size bowl sift together rye flour, all-purpose flour, baking powder, baking soda and salt. In a large bowl beat together buttermilk, oil, eggs, vodka and molasses. Gradually stir in flour mixture. Beat until smooth. Stir in caraway seeds. Lightly brush hot grids with shortening or oil. Pour enough batter to fill two-thirds of the waffle iron. Cook until crisp and golden-brown. While the waffles are cooking, prepare the Albacore Tuna Salad and preheat the broiler. Let finished waffles cool on a rack . Repeat with the remaining batter. To serve, cut waffles into quarter or half sections. Layer a tomato slice, a scoop of salad, alfalfa sprouts and some of the cheese on each section. Place assembled waffle sections under the broiler until cheese is slightly melted, 3 to 4 minutes. Makes about 4 waffles or 4 servings.

ALBACORE TUNA SALAD

In a large bowl combine tuna, mayonnaise, onion, bell pepper, salt, pepper and paprika. Stir until all ingredients are combined. Makes about 2 cups.

Curried Chicken Salad on Date, Nut & Fig Waffles

This is a unique idea that is wonderful to serve at luncheons. With fresh fruit on the side it's a sure winner. These waffles are so good that you can eat them with just a dab of cream cheese.

1-1/2 cups all-purpose flour
1/2 cup oat flour
1 tablespoon baking powder
1/4 teaspoon baking soda
1/2 teaspoon instant espresso coffee
2 eggs
1/4 cup packed light brown sugar
1/2 cup dairy sour cream
1-1/2 cups buttermilk
1 teaspoon vanilla extract
1/2 teaspoon almond extract
1/4 cup vegetable oil
1/2 cup chopped dates
1/2 cup dried figs, cut into small pieces

1/2 cup chopped walnuts
Vegetable shortening or oil for grids

CURRIED CHICKEN SALAD:

2 cups chicken breasts, boneless, skinless, cut into
    bite-size pieces
3/4 cup dairy sour cream
1/4 cup whipping cream
1 tablespoon curry powder
1 tablespoon lemon juice
2 Pippin apples, cored, finely diced
1/2 cup golden raisins
1/4 cup salted peanuts
1/4 cup finely diced celery
Salt and pepper to taste

Prepare the Curried Chicken Salad. Preheat waffle iron. Preheat oven to 250°F (120°C). In a medium-size bowl sift together all-purpose flour, oat flour, baking powder, baking soda and instant espresso. In a large bowl beat together eggs, brown sugar, sour cream, buttermilk, vanilla, almond extract and oil. Gradually stir in flour mixture. Beat until smooth. Stir in dates, figs and walnuts. Batter will be thick. Lightly brush hot grids with shortening or oil. Pour enough batter to fill two-thirds of the waffle iron. Push batter to the edges with a wooden spoon. Cook until crisp and golden-brown. Keep finished waffles warm in the oven on a rack until ready to serve. Repeat with the remaining batter. To serve, place a scoop of chilled salad on top of each waffle or waffle half. Makes about 4 waffles or 4 servings.

CURRIED CHICKEN SALAD

In a medium-size saucepan steam chicken pieces over boiling water until cooked, about 20 minutes. Set aside. In a large bowl blend together sour cream, whipping cream and curry powder. Sprinkle lemon juice over the apple pieces and add to cream mixture. Stir in cooked chicken pieces, raisins, peanuts and celery. Add salt and pepper. Toss until chicken is thoroughly coated. Cover and refrigerate 1 hour before serving. Makes about 3 cups.

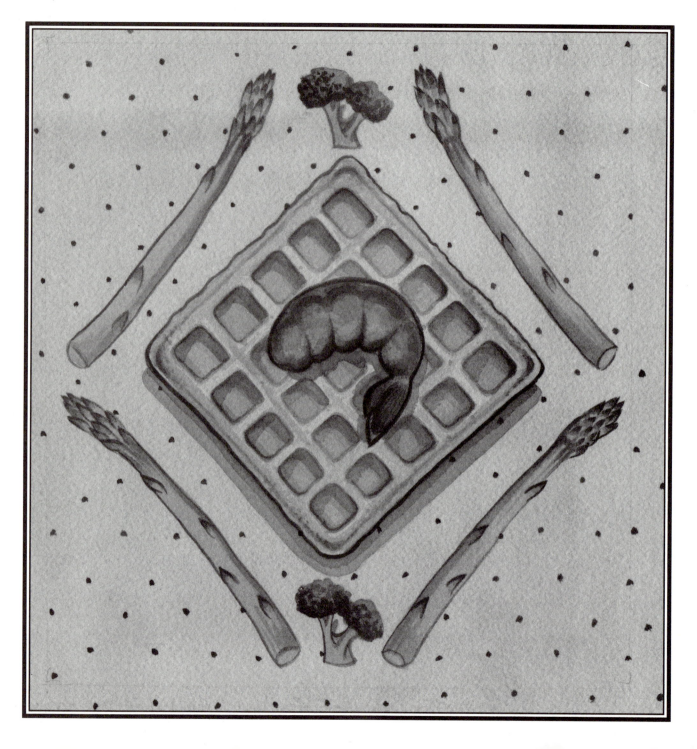

DINNER

Waffles are a scrumptious alternative to rice or noodles, especially when smothered with these delicious toppings. What better way to accentuate any entree than with tantalizing waffles made with sweet and spicy vegetable purees and served with a little butter as a side dish—a new way to eat your vegetables. Another time, substitute a hot waffle for dinner rolls. Any way you cut them, waffles can now be considered a square meal!

Beef Stroganoff on Crispy Waffles

Without a doubt, my husband makes the best Beef Stroganoff I've ever tasted, and I think this crispy waffle is one of the best waffles. That being the case, I think we've created the perfect combination between his stroganoff and my waffle!

1-3/4 cups milk
1 (1/4-oz.) package fast-rising yeast
2 cups all-purpose flour
1 teaspoon salt
1 teaspoon sugar
1/2 teaspoon baking soda
2 eggs
1/2 cup butter, melted, cooled
Vegetable shortening or oil for grids
Parsley for garnish

BEEF STROGANOFF:

2 pounds beef tenderloin

1/4 cup butter
1 cup chopped onion
1 garlic clove, minced
1/2 pound mushrooms, sliced (2 cups)
1-1/4 cups beef stock
2 tablespoons all-purpose flour
1 teaspoon salt
1/4 teaspoon pepper
1/2 teaspoon dried leaf tarragon
1/2 cup dry sherry
2 cups dairy sour cream

In a small saucepan slowly heat milk until warm to the touch, about 110°F (45°C). Transfer warmed milk to a small bowl. Add yeast and stir to dissolve. Set aside 5 minutes, until frothy. In a medium-size bowl sift together flour, salt, sugar and baking soda. In a large bowl beat together eggs and butter. Stir in yeast mixture. Gradually stir in flour mixture. Beat until smooth. Cover and let rest 10 minutes. Stir batter down. Cover and let rise 2 hours. After 1 hour prepare Beef Stroganoff. After batter has risen preheat waffle iron. Preheat oven to 250°F (120°C). Lightly brush hot grids with shortening or oil. Pour enough batter to fill two-thirds of the waffle iron. Cook until crisp and golden-brown. Keep finished waffles warm in the oven on a rack until ready to serve. Repeat with the remaining batter. Serve finished waffles whole or cut into halves. To serve, top generously with hot Beef Stroganoff and garnish with parsley. Makes about 4 waffles or 4 servings.

BEEF STROGANOFF

Trim fat from beef and cut crosswise into 1/2-inch strips. In a large skillet melt butter over low heat. Add onion, garlic and mushrooms; sauté until softened, about 5 minutes. Add meat and cook 10 minutes. Add 1 cup beef stock and cook on low heat 20 minutes. In a small jar shake together the remaining 1/4 cup of beef stock and flour until blended. Stir into skillet and add salt, pepper, tarragon, sherry and sour cream. Cook slowly until thick, about 10 minutes. Keep warm until ready to serve.

Shrimp Linden on Rice Waffles

This gourmet dish is one I love to serve when entertaining—simple and sophisticated.

1-1/3 cups water
1/2 cup rice
1 cup all-purpose flour
1 cup rice flour
1 tablespoon baking powder
1/2 teaspoon salt
1/4 teaspoon pepper
2 eggs
1-1/2 cups milk
Vegetable shortening or oil for grids
Parsley for garnish

SHRIMP LINDEN:

1/2 cup butter
2 garlic cloves, pressed

1 small onion, chopped
4 tomatoes, chopped
1 teaspoon chopped fresh basil
1 teaspoon minced fresh parsley
1 tablespoon sugar
1/4 teaspoon salt
1/4 teaspoon pepper
1/8 teaspoon dried leaf tarragon
1/2 cup dry white wine
1 cup whipping cream
1/4 cup all-purpose flour
1/2 teaspoon paprika
1-1/2 pounds bay shrimp, cooked

In a medium-size saucepan bring water to a boil. Stir in rice. Cover, reduce heat to low and simmer until all of the water is absorbed, 15 to 20 minutes. Set aside. In a medium-size bowl sift together all-purpose flour, rice flour, baking powder, salt and pepper. In a large bowl beat together eggs and milk. Gradually stir in flour mixture. Beat until smooth. Stir in cooked rice. Let batter stand while preparing Shrimp Linden. Batter will be thick. Preheat waffle iron. Preheat oven to 250°F (120°C). Lightly brush hot grids with shortening or oil. Pour enough batter to fill two-thirds of the waffle iron. Push batter to the sides with a wooden spoon. Cook until crisp and golden-brown. Keep finished waffles warm in the oven on a rack until ready to serve. Repeat with the remaining batter. Serve finished waffles whole or break into halves. To serve, top generously with hot Shrimp Linden. Garnish with parsley. Makes about 4 waffles or 4 servings.

SHRIMP LINDEN

In a large saucepan melt butter over low heat. Add garlic and onion. Sauté until the onion is softened. Add tomatoes. Cover and simmer 10 minutes. Add basil, parsley, sugar, salt, pepper, tarragon, wine and cream. Sprinkle in flour. Stir until blended. Cover and simmer 30 minutes. Stir occasionally. Sprinkle paprika over shrimp and stir into tomato sauce. Simmer 5 minutes.

Creamed Chicken on Sour-Cream Waffles

There is nothing worse than coming home from work tired, hungry and cranky, with very little desire to make a decent meal. Here is an easy, delicious solution to your dilemma. Simply good food fast!

2 cups all-purpose flour
1 tablespoon baking powder
1/2 teaspoon baking soda
1/4 teaspoon salt
1/8 teaspoon white pepper
1-1/4 cups dairy sour cream
1 cup milk
2 eggs, separated
1/3 cup vegetable oil
Vegetable shortening or oil for grids

CREAMED CHICKEN:

1/4 cup butter

3 tablespoons all-purpose flour
1/2 cup chicken stock
1/2 cup dairy sour cream
1 small onion, chopped
1 bay leaf
4 boneless skinless chicken breasts, cut into 1-inch
    pieces
1/2 cup sliced mushrooms
3 tablespoons chopped parsley
1 teaspoon Worcestershire sauce
1/2 teaspoon white pepper
1/2 teaspoon salt
1/2 cup small green peas, cooked

Prepare Creamed Chicken. Preheat waffle iron. Preheat oven to 250°F (120°C). In a medium-size bowl sift together flour, baking powder, baking soda, salt and pepper. In a large bowl beat together sour cream, milk, egg yolks and oil. Gradually stir in flour mixture. Beat until smooth. In a small bowl whip egg whites until soft peaks are formed. Fold into batter. Lightly brush hot grids with shortening or oil. Pour enough batter to fill two-thirds of the waffle iron. Cook until crisp and golden-brown. Keep finished waffles warm in the oven on a rack until ready to serve. Serve finished waffles whole or cut into halves. To serve, top generously with hot Creamed Chicken. Makes about 4 waffles or 4 servings.

CREAMED CHICKEN

In a large saucepan melt 2 tablespoons of the butter. Stir in flour, then chicken stock and sour cream until blended. Add onion and bay leaf. Reduce heat and simmer 10 minutes. In a medium-size skillet, melt remaining butter over low heat. Add chicken; sauté until almost cooked about 5 minutes. Remove cooked chicken from skillet. Stir into cream sauce. Add mushrooms, parsley, Worcestershire sauce, pepper, salt and peas. Cover and cook over low heat until ready to serve, 15 to 20 minutes, stirring occasionally. Do not boil. Discard bay leaf.

Veal Stew on Soothing Barley Waffles

Barley has a very subtle, nutlike flavor that is matched perfectly with this savory stew. But be careful barley is a natural relaxant. Which of course makes these perfect for a late-night meal.

1-3/4 cups milk
1 (1/4-oz.) package fast-rising yeast
1-1/2 cups barley flour
1/2 cup all-purpose flour
1/4 teaspoon baking soda
1/2 teaspoon salt
2 eggs
1/4 cup vegetable oil
Vegetable shortening or oil for grids

VEAL STEW:

3/4 cup butter
1/4 cup all-purpose flour
2 pounds boneless veal stew meat

1 cup chicken broth
3/4 cup whipping cream
1/2 cup dairy sour cream
1/2 cup dry sherry
2 teaspoons dried tarragon leaves
1/2 teaspoon dried sage leaves
1/2 teaspoon dried basil leaves
1/2 teaspoon salt
1/4 teaspoon pepper
1/2 teaspoon paprika
1 bay leaf
1 cup sliced mushrooms
1 shallot, chopped

In a small saucepan slowly heat milk until warm to the touch about 110°F (45°C). Transfer to a small bowl. Add yeast and stir to dissolve. Let stand 5 minutes, until frothy. In a medium-size bowl sift together barley flour, all-purpose flour, baking soda and salt. In a large bowl beat together eggs, oil and yeast mixture. Gradually stir in flour mixture. Beat until smooth. Cover and let rise in a warm place 2 hours. Prepare the Veal Stew. After the batter has risen preheat waffle iron. Preheat oven to 250°F (120°C). Lightly brush hot grids with shortening or oil. Pour enough batter to fill two-thirds of the waffle iron. Cook until crisp and golden-brown. Keep finished waffles warm in the oven on a rack until ready to serve. Repeat with the remaining batter. To serve, top hot waffles with Veal Stew. Makes about 4 waffles or 4 servings.

VEAL STEW

In a large saucepan melt butter over low heat. Lightly flour veal pieces. Sauté lightly in melted butter 5 minutes. In a small bowl blend together chicken broth, cream, sour cream and sherry. Pour over veal. Stir in tarragon, sage, basil, salt, pepper, paprika and bay leaf. Cover and simmer 40 to 45 minutes, stirring occasionally. Add mushrooms and shallot. Simmer until veal is tender, about 30 minutes. Discard bay leaf. Serve hot.

Spicy Broccoli Waffles with Vegetables & Cheese Sauce

These green gems are amazingly delicious, the perfect complement to grilled fish, chicken or steak. These waffles are also delectable for lunch with a salad or cut into rounds for an appetizer.

2 cups broccoli flowerets
1 cup all-purpose flour
1/2 cup whole-wheat pastry flour
1 tablespoon baking powder
1/2 teaspoon baking soda
3 tablespoons sugar
1/2 teaspoon salt
1/2 teaspoon red (cayenne) pepper
1/4 teaspoon garlic powder
1/4 teaspoon onion powder
1 cup buttermilk
1/4 cup vegetable oil
2 eggs, separated
1 tablespoon fresh lemon juice
Vegetable shortening or oil for grids
2 tablespoons finely chopped pimentos

STEAMED VEGETABLES:

1 pound small carrots, cut into 4-inch julienne strips
24 thin asparagus spears, cut into 4-inch lengths
3 large zucchini, cut into 4-inch wedges

CHEESE SAUCE:

2 tablespoons butter
1/2 teaspoon Dijon-style mustard
1/2 teaspoon salt
1/8 teaspoon paprika
1/4 teaspoon white pepper
1/2 cup half and half
1/2 cup dairy sour cream
1 cup shredded Cheddar cheese (4 ounces)
1 tablespoon dry sherry

In a medium-size saucepan cook broccoli in boiling water until soft, about 15 minutes. Drain; set aside. Preheat waffle iron. Preheat oven to 250°F (120°C). In a medium-size bowl sift together all-purpose flour, pastry flour, baking powder, baking soda, sugar, salt, cayenne, garlic powder and onion powder. In a blender or food processor fitted with the metal blade process cooked broccoli with 1/4 cup of the buttermilk until smooth. In a large bowl beat together remaining 3/4 cup of buttermilk, oil, egg yolks and lemon juice. Stir in broccoli puree. Gradually stir in flour. Beat until smooth. In a small bowl beat egg whites until soft peaks are formed. Fold into batter. Lightly brush hot grids with shortening or oil. Pour enough batter to fill half of the waffle iron. Cook until crisp and golden-brown. While the waffles are cooking, steam the vegetables and prepare Cheese Sauce. Keep finished waffles warm in the oven on a rack until ready to serve. Repeat with the remaining batter. To serve, cut waffles into quarter sections and place 3 to 4 pieces each of the steamed vegetables diagonally on each section. Cover with Cheese Sauce and sprinkle pimentos over the top. Serve immediately. Makes about 3 waffles or 4 servings.

STEAMED VEGETABLES

Steam vegetables over boiling water in a large saucepan until tender, about 10 minutes. Keep warm until ready to serve.

CHEESE SAUCE

In a small, heavy saucepan melt butter over low heat. Stir in mustard, salt, paprika, pepper, half and half and sour cream. Stir constantly until thickened. Add cheese and sherry. Stir until cheese is melted. Cover and simmer 3 minutes. Keep warm until ready to use. Makes about 1-1/2 cups.

Yellow-Squash Waffles with Ricotta-Cheese Topping

If you stretch your imagination, crooked neck yellow squash could look like geese walking in a row. In real life they whip up wonderfully to become a flavorful waffle that can be served with fantasylike results.

1 pound yellow crooked neck squash, cut into
　　1/2-inch pieces
1/4 cup dry plain bread crumbs
1 cup oat flour
1/2 cup all-purpose flour
2 tablespoons sugar
1-1/2 tablespoons baking powder
1/4 teaspoon baking soda
1/2 teaspoon salt
1/4 teaspoon lemon pepper

2 eggs, separated
1/2 cup buttermilk
1/2 cup dairy sour cream
1/3 cup butter, melted, cooled
2 tablespoons tarragon vinegar
1 tablespoon chopped parsley
Vegetable shortening or oil for grids
1 (15-oz.) container ricotta cheese
1/4 cup minced chives

Preheat waffle iron. Preheat oven to 250°F (120°C). In a large saucepan cook squash in boiling water until tender, about 5 minutes. Drain; set aside. In a large bowl stir together bread crumbs, oat flour, all-purpose flour, sugar, baking powder, baking soda, salt and lemon pepper. In a medium-size bowl beat together egg yolks, buttermilk and sour cream. In a blender or food processor fitted with the metal blade combine cooked squash, butter, vinegar, parsley and buttermilk mixture. Process until smooth. Stir into flour mixture. Beat until smooth. In a small bowl whip egg whites until soft peaks are formed. Fold into batter. Lightly brush hot grids with shortening or oil. Pour enough batter to fill two-thirds of the waffle iron. Cook until crisp and golden-brown. While the waffles are cooking, in a small bowl combine ricotta cheese and chives. Set aside. Keep finished waffles warm in the oven on a rack until ready to serve. Repeat with the remaining batter. To serve, cut waffles into quarter sections. Serve ricotta cheese and chives mixture on top. Serve hot. Makes about 3 waffles or 4 servings.

Buckwheat Waffles
with Asparagus & White-Wine Sauce

These waffles are so beautiful that they deserve to be served with the most elegant of meals. The green asparagus with a white ribbon of sauce running against the grey buckwheat is lovely, but most important of all they taste great!

1 cup milk
1 (1/4-oz.) package quick-rising yeast
1 cup buckwheat flour
1/2 cup all-purpose flour
1/4 teaspoon baking soda
1/2 teaspoon salt
2 tablespoons sugar
2 eggs, beaten
3 tablespoons vegetable oil

Vegetable shortening or oil for grids
24 thin asparagus spears, cut into 4-inch lengths
1/4 cup diced sun-dried tomatoes

WHITE-WINE SAUCE:

1 cup whipping cream
2 shallots, chopped
3/4 cup dry white wine
1/2 cup dairy sour cream
2 tablespoons all-purpose flour

In a small saucepan slowly heat milk until warm to the touch, about 110°F (45°C). Transfer to a small bowl. Add yeast and stir to dissolve. Set aside 5 minutes, until frothy. In a large bowl sift together buckwheat flour, all-purpose flour, baking soda, salt and sugar. Add yeast mixture, eggs and oil. Beat until smooth. Cover and let batter rise in a warm place 2 hours. After batter has risen preheat waffle iron. Preheat oven to 250°F (120°C). Lightly brush hot grids with shortening or oil. Ladle enough batter to fill one-third of each section of the waffle iron. (Do not overfill.) Cook until crisp and light brown. Keep finished waffles warm in the oven on a rack until ready to serve. While waffles are cooking, place asparagus in a large skillet. Cover with water. Bring to a boil, reduce heat and simmer 3 to 4 minutes, until tender. Prepare White-Wine Sauce. To serve, cut waffles into quarter sections, and place asparagus spears diagonally on each waffle section. Pour a ribbon of sauce over the top. Sprinkle sun-dried tomatoes over sauce. Serve immediately. Makes about 12 sections or 6 servings.

WHITE-WINE SAUCE

In a medium-size saucepan combine cream, shallots, white wine and sour cream. Warm slowly over low heat. Gradually stir in flour. Do not boil. Simmer until it starts to thicken, stirring occasionally. Keep warm until ready to serve. Makes about 2 cups.

Cheddar-Cheese Waffles

These crispy, cheesy waffles are great with chili, soup or any kind of entree. So delicious they don't need anything on top. The leftovers can be cut into 1-inch squares, sautéed in butter 1 minute and served as croutons!

3/4 cup all-purpose flour
1/2 cup oat flour
1 tablespoon baking powder
1/4 teaspoon baking soda
1 tablespoon sugar
1/2 teaspoon salt
2 eggs, separated

1/2 cup milk
1/2 cup buttermilk
1/4 cup vegetable oil
2 cups shredded sharp Cheddar cheese (8 ounces)
Vegetable shortening or oil for grids

Preheat waffle iron. Preheat oven to 250°F (120°C). In a medium-size bowl sift together all-purpose flour, oat flour, baking powder, baking soda, sugar and salt. In a large bowl beat together egg yolks, milk, buttermilk and oil. Gradually stir in flour mixture. Beat until smooth. Stir in Cheddar cheese. In a small bowl whip egg whites until soft peaks are formed. Fold into batter. Lightly brush hot grids with shortening or oil. Pour enough batter to fill three-quarters of the waffle iron. Cook until crisp and golden-brown. Keep finished waffles warm in the oven on a rack until ready to serve. Repeat with the remaining batter. To serve, cut waffles into quarter sections. Cut each quarter section in half. Serve hot. Makes about 2 waffles or 4 servings.

Herb Waffles

This versatile waffle is the quintessential alternative to the dinner roll. Serve proudly as you would any baked bread. Any leftovers can be processed in a blender for bread crumbs or cut into small pieces and sautéed in butter for croutons.

1-1/2 cups all-purpose flour
1-1/2 teaspoons baking powder
1/2 teaspoon baking soda
1/2 teaspoon salt
1 tablespoon dried leaf basil
1-1/4 teaspoons dried rosemary
1 teaspoon dried leaf oregano
1/4 teaspoon dried leaf thyme

1/4 teaspoon dried leaf tarragon
1/2 cup (4 ounces) cream cheese, softened
1-1/2 cups buttermilk
2 tablespoons olive oil
2 eggs
Olive oil for grids
1 cup butter, softened

Preheat waffle iron. Preheat oven to 250°F (120°C). In a medium-size bowl stir together flour, baking powder, baking soda, salt and herbs. In a large bowl beat together cream cheese, buttermilk, olive oil and eggs. Gradually stir in flour mixture. Beat until smooth. Lightly brush hot grids with olive oil. Pour enough batter to fill two-thirds of the waffle iron. Cook until crisp and golden-brown. Keep finished waffles warm in the oven on a rack until ready to serve. Repeat with the remaining batter. To serve, cut finished waffles into strips about 1 inch wide. Serve hot with butter. Makes about 3 waffles or 4 servings.

Carrot Waffles

These particular waffles are colorful, versatile, and their sweet and delicate flavor makes them an easy and unusual side dish. Serve for lunch, with a scoop of turkey salad, or as an appetizer cut into rounds and topped with sour cream. Cut finished waffles into rectangular pieces and make finger sandwiches with cream cheese and cucumber!

1 pound carrots, cut into 1-inch pieces	1 teaspoon ground nutmeg
1/4 cup milk	3/4 cup buttermilk
1 cup all-purpose flour	2 eggs, separated
1 cup oat flour	1/2 cup packed light brown sugar
1 tablespoon baking powder	1/4 cup vegetable oil
1/2 teaspoon baking soda	Vegetable shortening or oil for grids
1/2 teaspoon salt	1 cup dairy sour cream

Preheat waffle iron. Preheat oven to 250°F (120°C). In a medium-size saucepan cook carrots in boiling water until soft, about 15 minutes. Drain. In a blender or food processor fitted with the metal blade combine cooked carrots and milk. Process until smooth. Set aside. In a medium-size bowl, sift together all-purpose flour, oat flour, baking powder, baking soda, salt and nutmeg. In a large bowl beat together buttermilk, egg yolks, brown sugar, oil and carrot puree. Gradually stir in flour mixture. Beat until smooth. In a small bowl whip egg whites until soft peaks are formed. Fold into batter. Batter will be thick. Lightly brush hot grids with shortening or oil. Pour enough batter to fill two-thirds of the waffle iron. Push batter to the edges with a wooden spoon. Cook until crisp and golden-brown. Keep finished waffles warm in the oven on a rack until ready to serve. Repeat with the remaining batter. Cut waffles into quarter sections and serve with sour cream. Makes about 4 waffles or 4 servings.

Acorn-Squash Waffles

The texture of this waffle is light and crispy. Cut them into quarter sections, serve them with butter and they become a delightful change from steamed vegetables with dinner. The fennel seeds give these waffles an exotic licorice flavor.

2 acorn squash
1/3 cup milk
1 (1/4-oz.) package fast-rising yeast
1 cup oat flour
1/2 teaspoon baking soda
1/4 teaspoon salt
1 teaspoon curry powder
1 teaspoon ground ginger

1/4 teaspoon pepper
2 eggs, separated
1/4 cup butter, melted, cooled
1/4 cup packed light brown sugar
1/2 teaspoon fennel seeds
Vegetable shortening or oil for grids
1/2 cup butter, melted

Preheat oven to 350°F (175°C). Cut squash in halves and scrap out the seeds. Place squash on a baking sheet with the cut-sides down. Bake until tender, about 45 minutes. Squash can also be microwaved in a large microwave-safe dish with 1/2 cup water. Cover with plastic wrap and cook until tender, 10 minutes. Remove from the oven and allow to cool. In a small saucepan slowly heat milk until warm to the touch, about 110°F (45°C). Transfer to a small bowl. Add yeast and stir to dissolve. Let stand 5 minutes, until frothy. In a medium-size bowl sift together oat flour, baking soda, salt, curry powder, ginger and pepper. Scoop flesh from squash into a large bowl. Add eggs, the 1/4 cup butter, sugar and yeast mixture. Beat until all ingredients are blended. Gradually stir in flour mixture. Beat until smooth. Stir in fennel seeds. Cover and let rise in a warm place 2 hours. After batter has risen preheat waffle iron. Preheat oven to 250°F (120°C). Lightly brush hot grids with shortening or oil. Pour enough batter to fill two-thirds of the waffle iron. Cook until crisp and light brown. Keep finished waffles warm in the oven until ready to serve. To serve, cut finished waffles into quarter sections. Serve hot with melted butter on the side. Makes about 2 waffles or 4 servings.

Asparagus Waffles

The delicate flavor of these waffles will surprise everyone. Delicious along side any dinner entree or even cut into rounds for an appetizer. Who would have ever thought asparagus could come in squares?

2 cups (1-inch pieces) fresh asparagus
1 cup all-purpose flour
1 cup oat flour
1-1/2 tablespoons baking powder
1/4 teaspoon baking soda
1-1/2 teaspoons salt
1 teaspoon pepper
1/2 teaspoon ground nutmeg
1 teaspoon garlic powder

2 eggs, separated
1/2 cup milk
3/4 cup dairy sour cream
1/3 cup vegetable oil
1 tablespoon tarragon vinegar
1 tablespoon poppy seeds
Vegetable shortening or oil for grids
1 cup dairy sour cream

In a large saucepan cook asparagus in boiling water until tender 5 to 7 minutes. Drain. Preheat waffle iron. Preheat oven to 250°F (120°C). In a blender or food processor fitted with the metal blade process asparagus until smooth. In a medium-size bowl sift together all-purpose flour, oat flour, baking powder, baking soda, salt, pepper, nutmeg and garlic powder. In a large bowl beat together egg yolks, milk, sour cream, oil, tarragon vinegar and pureed asparagus. Gradually stir in flour mixture. Beat until smooth. Stir in poppy seeds. In a small bowl whip egg whites until soft peaks are formed. Fold into batter. Lightly brush hot grids with shortening or oil. Pour enough batter to fill two-thirds of the waffle iron. Cook until crisp and light brown. Keep finished waffles warm in the oven on a rack until ready to serve. Repeat with the remaining batter. To serve, cut waffles into quarter sections and top with sour cream. Serve immediately. Makes about 4 waffles or 4 servings.

DESSERTS

These waffles are everything your sweet tooth could ever desire: chocolately, chewy, nutty, gooey, sweet, tart and irresistible. Either cut the waffles with a cookie cutter or serve as quarters covered with delicious hot or cold syrups, sauces and sorbets. These imaginative treats are guaranteed to surprise and delight everyone.

Gingerbread Person Waffle with Old-Fashioned Icing

Now that manholes are person holes, manpower is people power and a chairman is a chairperson, let's welcome the gingerbread person! With these you're assured to please all the sexes. Choose either topping.

2 cups all-purpose flour
1 tablespoon baking powder
1/2 teaspoon baking soda
1/2 cup granulated sugar
1 tablespoon ground ginger
1-1/2 teaspoons ground cinnamon
3/4 teaspoon ground cloves
1/4 teaspoon ground nutmeg
Pinch of salt
1 cup milk
1/2 cup packed dark brown sugar
1/2 cup plain low-fat yogurt
2 tablespoons molasses
2 eggs, separated
1/4 cup vegetable oil
1/4 cup butter, melted, for grids

OLD-FASHIONED WHITE ICING (OPTIONAL):

1-1/2 cups powdered sugar
1 egg white
1 teaspoon vanilla extract
2 tablespoons milk
1/4 cup butter, softened
1 tablespoon light corn syrup

APPLE-CINNAMON TOPPING (OPTIONAL):

1/2 cup butter
1 tablespoon lemon juice
4 Golden Delicious apples, peeled, cored, cut
  into bite-size pieces
1/3 cup packed dark brown sugar
1/4 teaspoon ground cinnamon
1/8 teaspoon ground ginger
1/8 teaspoon ground nutmeg
1/4 cup walnuts, chopped
1 cup whipping cream

Preheat waffle iron. Preheat oven to 250°F (120°C). In a medium-size bowl sift together flour, baking powder, baking soda, granulated sugar, ginger, cinnamon, cloves, nutmeg and salt. In a large bowl beat together milk, brown sugar, yogurt, molasses, egg yolks and oil. Gradually stir in flour mixture. Beat until smooth. Lightly brush hot grids with melted butter. Pour enough batter to fill two-thirds of the waffle iron. Cook until crisp and a rich brown. Repeat with the remaining batter. While the waffles are cooking, prepare the icing or topping. To serve waffles with icing, let waffles cool slightly on a rack, then cut with a gingerbread person cookie cutter. Spread a thin layer of icing over the top. To serve waffles with the topping, keep finished waffles warm in the oven until ready to serve. Cut waffles into quarter sections and spoon hot topping and whipped cream over waffles. Makes about 4 waffles or about 16 cookies.

OLD-FASHIONED WHITE ICING

In a medium-size bowl combine powdered sugar, egg white, vanilla, milk, butter and corn syrup. With an electric mixer on low speed beat until all ingredients are blended and icing is smooth without any lumps. Keep refrigerated until ready to serve. Makes about 1/3 cup.

APPLE-CINNAMON TOPPING

In a medium-size saucepan melt butter. Sprinkle lemon juice over the apple pieces. Stir into melted butter. Stir in sugar, spices and walnuts. Cook slowly over low heat, stirring occasionally, until apples are golden-brown, about 10 minutes. Cover. Keep warm until ready to serve. Makes about 2 cups. In a small bowl whip cream until soft peaks are formed. Keep refrigerated until ready to serve.

Layer-Cake Waffles with Berries & Pudding

These individual layer cakes are delicious, look charming and are simple to prepare. Wonderful for small dinner parties because they're "real show stoppers!" The perfect ending to the perfect evening.

1 (3-oz.) package instant vanilla pudding
1-1/2 cups all-purpose flour
1/2 teaspoon baking powder
1/4 teaspoon baking soda
1/4 teaspoon salt
3/4 cup sugar
3/4 cup milk
1/2 cup half and half
2 eggs, separated
3 tablespoons butter, melted, cooled

1 tablespoon fresh lemon juice
1 teaspoon vanilla extract
Vegetable shortening or oil for grids
1 cup whipping cream
1 cup strawberries, fresh or frozen, thawed, sliced
1 cup blackberries, fresh or frozen, thawed

ORANGE-MARMALADE SAUCE:

3/4 cup orange marmalade
1/2 cup hot water

Prepare instant pudding according to package instructions. Chill until ready to serve. Preheat waffle iron. Preheat oven to 250°F (120°C). In a medium-size bowl sift together flour, baking powder, baking soda, salt and sugar. In a large bowl beat together milk, half and half, egg yolks, butter, lemon juice and vanilla. Gradually stir in flour mixture. Beat until smooth. In a small bowl whip egg whites until soft peaks are formed. Fold into batter. Lightly brush hot grids with shortening or oil. Pour enough batter to fill two-thirds of the waffle iron. Cook until crisp and golden-brown. While the waffles are cooking, prepare the Orange-Marmalade Sauce. Keep finished waffles warm in the oven on a rack until ready to serve. Repeat with the remaining batter. In a small bowl whip cream until soft peaks are formed. Keep refrigerated until ready to serve. To assemble, cut finished waffles into quarter sections. Each serving will use three sections. First spread a thick layer of vanilla pudding on one section. Next place a few strawberry slices on top of vanilla pudding. Place a waffle section on top of strawberries. On this second section spread another thick layer of vanilla pudding and place a few blackberries. Place the third waffle section on top of blackberries. Pour about 3 tablespoons of hot Orange-Marmalade Sauce over the top and let it drip down the sides. Spoon whipped cream on top. Makes about 3 waffles or 4 servings.

ORANGE-MARMALADE SAUCE

In a medium-size saucepan warm orange marmalade with water over low heat. Simmer until small bubbles appear around the edges, stirring occasionally. Do not boil. Keep warm until ready to serve. Makes about 1-1/2 cups.

Chocolate Fudge Brownie Waffles

This is without a doubt one of the best waffles in the world! If you want a waffle that is rich, moist, chocolatey and nutty, this is the one for you. Serve with powdered sugar or with ice cream, chocolate fudge sauce and whipped cream if you dare!

4 ounces unsweetened chocolate
1/3 cup butter
1-1/2 cups all-purpose flour
1 tablespoon baking powder
1/2 teaspoon baking soda
1/2 cup granulated sugar
1 tablespoon unsweetened cocoa powder

3 eggs, separated
1/2 cup milk
1/2 cup dairy sour cream
1 teaspoon vanilla extract
3/4 cup walnuts, chopped
Vegetable shortening or oil for grids
Powdered sugar

Preheat waffle iron. Preheat oven to 250°F (120°C). In a small, heavy saucepan or double boiler melt chocolate and butter over low heat. In a medium-size bowl sift together flour, baking powder, baking soda, granulated sugar and cocoa powder. In a large bowl beat together egg yolks, milk, sour cream and vanilla. Gradually stir in flour mixture and melted chocolate and butter. Beat until smooth. Stir in walnuts. In a small bowl whip egg whites until soft peaks are formed. Fold into batter. Batter will be thick. Lightly brush hot grids with shortening or oil. Pour enough batter to fill two-thirds of the waffle iron. Push batter out to the edges with a wooden spoon. Cook until crisp and a dark rich brown. Be careful not to overcook. Keep finished waffles warm in the oven on a rack until ready to serve. Repeat with the remaining batter. To serve cut waffles into quarter sections. Sprinkle powdered sugar through a fine sieve over the top. Makes about 3 waffles or 4 servings.

Mom's Lemon Pie Waffles with Whipped Cream

Every summer for one of our big family gatherings, my mom makes a sensational lemon cream pie with lemons picked fresh right off the backyard tree. It's everyone's favorite, and I think this waffle does it proud.

1 cup all-purpose flour
1 tablespoon baking powder
1/2 cup powdered sugar
1/2 cup sweetened condensed milk
1/4 cup milk
2 egg yolks
1/4 teaspoon vanilla extract
3 tablespoons vegetable oil

3/4 cup fresh lemon juice
1/4 cup grated lemon zest
3 egg whites
Vegetable shortening or oil for grids
1 cup whipping cream
1/4 cup granulated sugar
Mint sprigs for garnish

Preheat waffle iron. Preheat oven to 250°F (120°C). In a medium-size bowl sift together flour, baking powder and powdered sugar. In a large bowl beat together condensed milk, milk, egg yolks, vanilla, oil and lemon juice. Gradually stir in flour mixture. Beat until smooth. Stir in lemon zest. In a small bowl beat egg whites until soft peaks are formed. Fold into batter. Lightly brush hot grids with shortening or oil. Ladle enough batter to fill two-thirds of each section of the waffle iron. (Do not overfill.) Cook until crisp and golden-brown. While waffles are cooking, in a small bowl whip together cream and granulated sugar until soft peaks are formed. Keep refrigerated until ready to serve. Keep finished waffles warm in the oven on a rack until ready to serve. Repeat with the remaining batter. To serve, cut waffles into quarter sections. Serve waffles hot with whipped cream on top. Garnish with mint sprigs. Makes about 12 sections or 6 servings.

S'Waffles

Every camper has a soft spot in his or her heart for this wonderful treat. No need to build a campfire, these waffles can be enjoyed in the warmth of the kitchen even on a rainy day.

12 (2-1/2-inch) graham cracker squares
3/4 cup all-purpose flour
1/2 cup sugar
1 tablespoon baking powder
1/4 teaspoon baking soda
1 teaspoon ground cinnamon
2 eggs, separated
3/4 cup milk
1/2 cup plain low-fat yogurt
1/4 cup butter, melted, cooled
1/4 teaspoon vanilla extract

Vegetable shortening or oil for grids
24 large marshmallows

CHOCOLATE SAUCE:

1 cup semisweet chocolate chips
1 tablespoon butter
1/4 cup sugar
3/4 cup whipping cream
1 teaspoon vanilla extract
1 tablespoon unsweetened cocoa powder

Preheat waffle iron. In a blender or food processor fitted with the metal blade process graham crackers until they form fine crumbs. In a medium-size bowl whisk together graham cracker crumbs, flour, sugar, baking powder, baking soda and cinnamon. In a large bowl beat together egg yolks, milk, yogurt, butter and vanilla. Gradually stir in flour mixture. Beat until smooth. In a small bowl whip egg whites until soft peaks are formed. Fold into batter. Lightly brush hot grids with shortening or oil. Pour enough batter to fill two-thirds of the waffle iron. Cook until crisp and golden-brown. While the waffles are cooking, prepare the Chocolate Sauce and preheat the broiler. Keep finished waffles on a rack until ready to serve. Repeat with the remaining batter. To serve, cut waffles into quarter sections. Divide marshmallows among sections. Place under the broiler until marshmallows start to turn light brown 2 to 3 minutes. Remove from heat and pour hot Chocolate Sauce over the top. Serve immediately. Makes about 3 waffles or 6 servings.

CHOCOLATE SAUCE

In a small saucepan or double boiler melt chocolate and butter together over low heat. Stir in sugar, cream, vanilla and cocoa powder. Simmer until sugar is dissolved, stirring occasionally. Do not boil. Keep warm until ready to serve. Makes about 1-1/2 cups.

Butterscotch Waffles with Gingered Pears

Butterscotch is a wonderful flavor that everyone enjoys. And now this simple taste has been elevated to new heights with the addition of Gingered Pears, together they melt in your mouth.

1-1/2 cups all-purpose flour
1 tablespoon baking powder
1/2 cup whipping cream
3/4 cup milk
1 teaspoon vanilla extract
1/3 cup butter, melted, cooled
2 eggs, separated
1/2 cup packed dark brown sugar
1/2 cup butterscotch chips
Vegetable shortening or oil for grids
1/4 cup powdered sugar

GINGERED PEARS:

3 tablespoons butter
3/4 cup packed light brown sugar
1 teaspoon ground ginger
2 ripe Anjou pears, peeled, sliced lengthwise into
    1/4-inch-wide pieces
1/4 cup whipping cream
2 tablespoons brandy

Preheat waffle iron. Preheat oven to 250°F (120°C). In a small bowl sift together flour and baking powder. In a large bowl beat together cream, milk, vanilla, butter, egg yolks and brown sugar. Gradually stir in flour mixture. Beat until smooth. Stir in butterscotch chips. In a small bowl whip egg whites until soft peaks are formed. Fold into batter. Lightly brush hot grids with shortening or oil. Pour enough batter to fill two-thirds of the waffle iron. Cook until crisp and golden-brown. While the waffles are cooking prepare the Gingered Pears. Keep finished waffles warm in the oven on a rack until ready to serve. Repeat with the remaining batter. To serve, cut waffles into quarter sections. Place Gingered Pears on each waffle section and spoon hot sauce over the top. Sprinkle powdered sugar through a fine sieve over the top. Serve immediately. Makes about 3 waffles or 6 servings.

GINGERED PEARS

In a large skillet melt butter over low heat. Add sugar and ginger. Stir until sugar is dissolved and small bubbles appear around the edges. Do not boil. Carefully add sliced pears. Turn occasionally. Stir in cream and brandy. Simmer until pears are tender about 5 minutes. Serve hot.

Vanilla Gorilla Waffles
with Vanilla & Raspberry Sauces

As I have spent many hours in the kitchen, I have developed a strong friendship with the stuffed gorilla that sits prominently on the water cooler. We have discussed many of the recipes as well as world events and I truly value his opinion. And so it is to you, my fine furry friend, that I dedicate this glorious waffle!

3/4 cup milk
1/4 cup whipping cream
1 vanilla bean
1-1/2 cups all-purpose flour
3/4 cup sugar
1 tablespoon baking powder
1/2 teaspoon baking soda
2 eggs, separated
1 teaspoon vanilla extract
1/2 cup vanilla-flavored low-fat yogurt
2 tablespoons vegetable shortening, melted,
    cooled
1/2 teaspoon fresh lemon juice

1/4 teaspoon cream of tartar
Vegetable shortening or oil for grids
1 quart vanilla ice cream

VANILLA SAUCE:

1 cup whipping cream
1/2 cup vanilla chips
1/2 teaspoon almond extract

RASPBERRY SAUCE:

2 cups raspberries, fresh or frozen, thawed,
    drained
2 tablespoons sugar
1 tablespoon raspberry liqueur

Preheat waffle iron. Preheat oven to 250°F (120°C). In a small saucepan slowly warm milk and cream over low heat. Cut the vanilla bean in half lengthwise and scrape all the contents of the bean into the warm milk mixture. When the milk mixture comes to a simmer, remove from heat. Cover and let stand 1 hour. In a medium-size bowl, sift together flour, sugar, baking powder and baking soda. In a large bowl, beat together egg yolks, vanilla, yogurt, shortening and lemon juice. Add milk mixture. Gradually stir in flour mixture. Beat until smooth. In a small bowl whip egg whites with cream of tartar until soft peaks are formed. Fold into batter. Lightly brush hot grids with shortening or oil. Pour enough batter to fill two-thirds of the waffle iron. Cook until crisp and golden-brown. Keep finished waffles warm in the oven on a rack until ready to serve. Repeat with the remaining batter. While the waffles are cooking prepare Vanilla and Raspberry Sauces. To serve, cut waffles into quarter or half sections. Place 1 scoop of ice cream on each section and pour Vanilla Sauce over the top and around the sides. Pour a small amount of Raspberry Sauce on top of the Vanilla Sauce, letting it drip down the sides. Very carefully put dots of Raspberry Sauce in the Vanilla Sauce that is around the waffles on the plates, forming a border of red dots floating in the Vanilla Sauce. Serve immediately. Makes about 3 waffles or 4 servings.

VANILLA SAUCE

In a small, heavy saucepan or double boiler heat cream and vanilla chips over low heat, stirring occasionally until smooth. Add almond extract. Do not boil. Keep warm until ready to serve. Just before serving transfer sauce to a container with an easy pouring spout. Makes about 1-1/4 cups.

RASPBERRY SAUCE

In a blender or food processor fitted with the metal blade process raspberries until smooth. Gradually stir in sugar and liqueur and continue to process until blended. Transfer to a container with an easy pouring spout. Makes about 1 cup.

Peach Cobbler Waffles

My grandmother used to hide gifts for me in her luggage, take me shopping for the right outfit and instruct me on how nice girls were to behave. Twice a year she would come to California to visit us, and always baked a peach cobbler.

1-3/4 cups all-purpose flour
1 tablespoon baking powder
1/2 teaspoon baking soda
1/4 teaspoon salt
1/2 cup sugar
1/2 cup milk
3/4 cup half and half
1/2 teaspoon vanilla extract
2 egg yolks

2 tablespoons vegetable oil
3 egg whites
1 tablespoon ground cinnamon
Vegetable shortening or oil for grids
1 cup whipping cream

PEACH COBBLER TOPPING:

2 cups sliced peaches, fresh or frozen,
  thawed, drained
1/2 cup sugar

Preheat waffle iron. Preheat oven to 250°F (120°C). In a medium-size bowl sift together flour, baking powder, baking soda, salt and 1/4 cup of the sugar. In a large bowl beat together milk, half and half, vanilla, egg yolks and oil. Gradually stir in flour mixture. Beat until smooth. In a small bowl whip egg whites until soft peaks are formed. Fold into batter. In a small bowl combine remaining 1/4 cup of sugar and the cinnamon. Set aside. Lightly brush hot grids with shortening or oil. Pour enough batter to fill two-thirds of the waffle iron. Cook until barely crisp about 3 minutes. Raise the lid and sprinkle 2 tablespoons of the cinnamon mixture over the top. Cook until crisp and golden-brown. While the waffles are cooking, prepare Peach Topping, and in a small bowl whip cream until soft peaks are formed. Keep refrigerated until ready to serve. Keep finished waffles warm in the oven on a rack until ready to serve. Repeat with the remaining batter. Do not stack finished waffles. To serve, cut waffles into quarter sections. Cover each section with hot Peach Cobbler Topping. Spoon whipped cream on top. Serve immediately. Makes about 3 waffles or 6 servings.

PEACH COBBLER TOPPING

In a medium-size saucepan combine peaches and sugar. Simmer on low heat until tender about 10 minutes, stirring occasionally. Keep warm until ready to serve. Makes about 2 cups.

Peppermint Waffles
with Peppermint Whipped Cream

With such an enchanting taste and color, you'll swear they're red and white striped! This pretty pink waffle is filled with flavor and, when topped with whipped cream and candy pieces, makes for a striking dessert.

1-1/2 cups all-purpose flour
1 tablespoon baking powder
1/3 cup sugar
2 eggs, separated
1 cup milk
1/2 cup whipping cream
1 teaspoon peppermint extract
2 tablespoons vegetable oil

1/4 cup peppermint candies, crushed
Vegetable shortening or oil for grids
1/4 cup peppermint candies, broken

PEPPERMINT WHIPPED CREAM:

1 cup whipping cream
1 teaspoon peppermint extract
1/2 cup powdered sugar
1 drop red food coloring

Preheat waffle iron. Preheat oven to 250°F (120°C). In a medium-size bowl sift together flour, baking powder and sugar. In a large bowl beat together egg yolks, milk, cream, peppermint extract and oil. Gradually stir in flour mixture. Beat until smooth. Stir in crushed peppermint candies. In a small bowl whip egg whites until soft peaks are formed. Fold into batter. Lightly brush hot grids with shortening or oil. Pour enough batter to fill two-thirds of the waffle iron. Cook until crisp and golden-brown. While the waffles are cooking, prepare Peppermint Whipped Cream. Keep finished waffles warm in the oven on a rack until ready to serve. Repeat with the remaining batter. To serve cut waffles into quarter sections. Spoon Peppermint Whipped Cream on top. Sprinkle broken peppermint candies over the top. Makes about 3 waffles or 6 servings.

PEPPERMINT WHIPPED CREAM

In a small bowl combine cream, peppermint extract, powdered sugar and red food coloring. Whip until soft peaks are formed. Keep refrigerated until ready to serve. Makes about 1-1/2 cups.

Carrot Cake Waffles with Cream-Cheese Icing

With just the right amount of spices and sweetness these will delight everyone's taste buds, even traditional carrot cake lovers. For the cook they're wonderful, because they're easy to prepare and they taste like you've cooked for days.

2 bunches carrots (1-1/2 pounds total)
1-1/2 cups all-purpose flour
1-1/2 tablespoons baking powder
1/2 teaspoon baking soda
1/2 teaspoon salt
1 teaspoon ground cinnamon
1/2 cup milk
1/2 cup dairy sour cream
2 eggs, separated
1/3 cup vegetable oil

1 teaspoon vanilla extract
1/2 cup packed light brown sugar
1/2 cup pecans, chopped
Vegetable shortening or oil for grids
1 quart vanilla ice cream

CREAM-CHEESE ICING:

1 (8-oz.) package cream cheese, softened
1/4 cup butter, softened
2-1/2 cups powdered sugar
1 tablespoon vanilla extract

Peel and shred 1 bunch of carrots; set aside. Cut the remaining bunch of carrots into 1-inch pieces. In a medium-size saucepan cook carrot pieces in boiling water until tender 5 to 7 minutes. Drain. In a blender or food processor fitted with the metal blade process cooked carrot pieces until smooth. Set aside. Preheat waffle iron. Preheat oven to 250°F (120°C). In a medium-size bowl sift together flour, baking powder, baking soda, salt and cinnamon. In a large bowl beat together milk, sour cream, egg yolks, oil, vanilla, brown sugar and pureed carrots. Gradually stir in flour mixture. Beat until smooth. Stir in shredded carrots and pecans. In a small bowl whip egg whites until soft peaks are formed. Fold into batter. Lightly brush hot grids with shortening or oil. Pour enough batter to fill two-thirds of the waffle iron. Cook until crisp and golden-brown. While the waffles are cooking prepare the Cream-Cheese Icing. Keep finished waffles warm in the oven on a rack until ready to serve. Repeat with the remaining batter. To serve, cut waffles into quarter sections. Spread a thick layer of Cream-Cheese Icing on top of each hot waffle section and place a scoop of vanilla ice cream on the side. Makes about 3 waffles or 6 servings.

CREAM-CHEESE ICING

In a medium-size bowl combine cream cheese, butter, sugar and vanilla. With an electric mixer on low speed beat until all ingredients are well blended. Keep refrigerated until ready to serve. Makes about 1-1/2 cups.

Dutch Apple Spice Waffles

The inviting aroma of these waffles is guaranteed to fill your head with all kinds of wonderful memories, and they will fill your tummy!

1-1/2 cups all-purpose flour
1-1/2 tablespoons baking powder
1/4 teaspoon baking soda
1/4 teaspoon salt
1 teaspoon ground cinnamon
1/2 teaspoon ground nutmeg
1/2 teaspoon ground cloves
1/4 teaspoon ground ginger
1/4 teaspoon ground mace
2 eggs, separated
1 cup buttermilk

1/4 cup apple cider
1/4 cup dairy sour cream
1 tablespoon fresh lemon juice
1 teaspoon vanilla extract
1/3 cup butter, melted, cooled
1/3 cup packed dark brown sugar
1/4 cup pecans, finely chopped
2 cups Granny Smith apples, cored, chopped
1/2 cup currants
Vegetable shortening or oil for grids
1 quart vanilla ice cream

Preheat waffle iron. Preheat oven to 250°F (120°C). In a medium-size bowl sift together flour, baking powder, baking soda, salt and spices. In a large bowl beat together egg yolks, buttermilk, apple cider, sour cream, lemon juice, vanilla, butter and brown sugar. Gradually stir in flour mixture. Beat until smooth. Stir in pecans, apple pieces and currants. Lightly brush hot grids with shortening or oil. Pour enough batter to fill two-thirds of the waffle iron. Push batter to the edges with a wooden spoon. Cook until crisp and golden-brown. Keep finished waffles warm in the oven on a rack until ready to serve. Repeat with the remaining batter. To serve, cut waffles into quarter sections. Serve hot with a scoop of vanilla ice cream on top. Makes about 3 waffles or 6 servings.

Coconut Macaroon Waffles

These waffles lend themselves perfectly to a whole array of toppings, including different flavors of ice creams or fresh fruit for a lighter dessert. And of course because they taste like fresh baked macaroons they're great just by themselves.

1-1/4 cups all-purpose flour
1 tablespoon baking powder
1/2 cup sugar
1/4 teaspoon salt
2 eggs, separated
1/2 cup half and half
1/4 cup milk
1-1/4 teaspoons coconut extract

1/2 teaspoon almond extract
1/4 cup vegetable oil
1 cup flaked coconut
Vegetable shortening or oil for grids
1 cup whipping cream
1/4 cup sugar
Mint sprigs for garnish

Preheat waffle iron. Preheat oven to 250°F (120°C). In a medium-size bowl sift together flour, baking powder, sugar and salt. In a large bowl beat together egg yolks, half and half, milk, coconut extract, almond extract and oil. Gradually stir in flour mixture. Beat until smooth. Stir in 1/2 cup of the coconut. In a small bowl whip egg whites until soft peaks are formed. Fold into batter. Lightly brush grids with shortening or oil. Ladle enough batter to fill 1/2 of each quarter section of the waffle iron. (Do not overfill.) Sprinkle about 1 tablespoon of the remaining coconut over the top of the batter. Cook until crisp and golden-brown. While the waffles are cooking, in a small bowl whip together cream and sugar until soft peaks are formed. Keep refrigerated until ready to serve. Keep finished waffles warm in the oven on a rack until ready to serve. To serve, cut waffles into quarter sections. Place a spoonful of whipped cream on top of each section. Sprinkle with remaining coconut. Garnish with mint sprigs. Makes about 12 sections or 6 servings.

Angel Food Cake Waffles with Raspberry-Peach Sauce

These waffles have captured this devilishly delicious taste perfectly. But when topped with the Raspberry-Peach Sauce they become absolutely heavenly!

1-1/2 cups all-purpose flour
1-1/4 cups superfine sugar
1 tablespoon baking powder
1/4 teaspoon baking soda
1/4 teaspoon salt
1/2 cup half and half
1/2 cup whipping cream
1-1/2 teaspoons vanilla extract
1/2 teaspoon almond extract
3/4 teaspoon fresh lemon juice

1/4 cup vegetable oil
3 egg yolks
4 egg whites
1/2 teaspoon cream of tartar
Vegetable shortening or oil for grids
Powdered sugar

RASPBERRY-PEACH SAUCE:

1 (12-oz.) package frozen raspberries, thawed
1 (12-oz.) package frozen peaches, thawed
1/2 cup hot water

Preheat waffle iron. In a medium-size bowl sift together flour, superfine sugar, baking powder, baking soda and salt. In a large bowl beat together half and half, cream, vanilla, almond extract, lemon juice, oil and egg yolks. Gradually stir in flour mixture. Beat until smooth. In a small bowl whip egg whites with cream of tartar until soft peaks are formed. Fold into batter. Lightly brush hot grids with shortening or oil. Pour enough batter to fill three-quarters of the waffle iron. Cook until crisp and light brown. Be careful not to overcook. While the waffles are cooking, prepare Raspberry-Peach Sauce. Let finished waffles cool on a rack. Repeat with the remaining batter. To serve cut waffles into quarter sections. Pour hot Raspberry-Peach Sauce over the top. Sprinkle powdered sugar through a fine sieve over the top. Serve immediately. Makes about 3 waffles or 6 servings.

RASPBERRY-PEACH SAUCE

In a medium-size saucepan or double boiler combine raspberries, peaches and water. Simmer over low heat until the raspberries start to break apart, and small bubbles start to appear around the edges. Simmer 5 minutes, stirring occasionally. Keep warm until ready to serve. Makes about 2 cups.

Peanut Brittle Waffles with Gingered Apples

For someone with a sweet tooth this candylike waffle is gooey, chewy, crunchy and yummy. Something into which you will really want to sink your teeth.

1-1/4 cups all-purpose flour
1/2 cup oat flour
1 tablespoon baking powder
1/4 teaspoon baking soda
1/4 teaspoon salt
2 eggs
3/4 cup milk
1/4 cup butter, melted, cooled
3/4 cup packed light brown sugar
1/2 teaspoon vanilla extract

1 cup crushed peanut brittle candy
1/2 cup salted peanuts, chopped
Melted butter for grids

GINGERED APPLES:

1-1/4 cups butter
1/2 teaspoon vanilla extract
1 tablespoon ground ginger
1/2 cup packed dark brown sugar
4 Granny Smith apples, peeled, cored, diced

Preheat waffle iron. Preheat oven to 250°F (120°C). In a medium-size bowl sift together all-purpose flour, oat flour, baking powder, baking soda and salt. In a large bowl beat together eggs, milk, butter, sugar and vanilla. Gradually stir in flour mixture. Beat until smooth. Stir in peanut brittle and peanuts. Lightly brush hot grids with butter. Pour enough batter to fill two-thirds of the waffle iron. Cook until crisp and golden-brown. While the waffles are cooking, prepare the Gingered Apples. Keep finished waffles warm in the oven on a rack until ready to serve. Repeat with the remaining batter. To serve cut waffles into quarter or half sections. Spoon hot apples over the top. Serve immediately. Makes about 4 waffles or 6 servings.

GINGERED APPLES

In a medium-size saucepan melt butter over low heat. Add vanilla, ginger, sugar and apple pieces. Stir constantly until apple pieces are covered with ginger sauce. Cook until apples are soft and start to turn a light brown about 10 minutes, stirring occasionally. Keep warm until ready to serve. Makes about 2 cups.

Cappuccino Waffles with Hazelnut Sauce

With a rich coffee taste that is not too strong, these wonderful waffles with coffee ice cream and Hazelnut Sauce are addicting! But don't worry they won't keep you up nights!

1-1/4 cups all-purpose flour
1 tablespoon baking powder
3/4 cup powdered sugar
1/4 cup instant espresso coffee
2 eggs, separated
1/2 cup milk
1/4 cup buttermilk
1/4 cup whipping cream
1 teaspoon vanilla extract
1/4 cup vegetable oil

Vegetable shortening or oil for grids
1 quart coffee-flavored ice cream

HAZELNUT SAUCE:

1 tablespoon butter
1/2 cup whipping cream
1/4 cup powdered sugar
1 teaspoon Kahlúa liqueur
1 tablespoon Frangelico liqueur
1/4 teaspoon almond extract
2 tablespoons finely chopped hazelnuts

Preheat waffle iron. Preheat oven to 250°F (120°C). In a medium-size bowl sift together flour, baking powder, powdered sugar and instant espresso. In a large bowl beat together egg yolks, milk, buttermilk, cream, vanilla and oil. Gradually stir in flour mixture. Beat until smooth. In a small bowl whip egg whites until soft peaks are formed. Fold into batter. Lightly brush hot grids with shortening or oil. Pour enough batter to fill two-thirds of the waffle iron. Cook until crisp and a rich brown. While the waffles are cooking, prepare the Hazelnut Sauce. Keep finished waffles warm in the oven on a rack until ready to serve. Repeat with the remaining batter. To serve, cut waffles into quarter sections. Place a scoop of ice cream on top of each section. Pour a ribbon of hot Hazelnut Sauce over the top. Serve immediately. Makes about 2 waffles or 4 servings.

HAZELNUT SAUCE

In a small saucepan melt butter over low heat. Stir in cream, sugar, liqueurs, almond extract and hazelnuts. Simmer 3 to 4 minutes, stirring occasionally. Do not boil. Keep warm until ready to serve. Makes about 3/4 cup.

Strawberry Short-Waffles

Like old-fashioned strawberry shortcake this dessert is sure to be a summertime favorite.

1-1/4 cups all-purpose flour
1-1/2 tablespoons baking powder
1/2 teaspoon baking soda
1/2 cup sugar
1/4 teaspoon salt
1/2 cup milk
1/2 cup whipping cream
2 eggs, separated

1 teaspoon vanilla extract
1/8 teaspoon almond extract
1/3 cup butter, melted, cooled
1/4 teaspoon cream of tartar
Vegetable shortening or oil for grids
1 cup whipping cream
2 tablespoons sugar
2 cups fresh strawberries, halved, chilled

Preheat waffle iron. Preheat oven to 250°F (120°C). In a medium-size bowl sift together flour, baking powder, baking soda, the 1/2 cup sugar and salt. In a large bowl beat together milk, cream, egg yolks, vanilla, almond extract and butter. Gradually stir in flour mixture. Beat until smooth. In a small bowl whip egg whites and cream of tartar until soft peaks are formed. Fold into batter. Batter will be thick. Lightly brush hot grids with shortening or oil. Pour enough batter to fill two-thirds of the waffle iron. Push batter to the edges with a wooden spoon. Cook until crisp and golden-brown. While the waffles are cooking, in a small bowl whip together cream and the 2 tablespoons sugar until soft peaks are formed. Keep refrigerated until ready to serve. Keep finished waffles warm in the oven on a rack until ready to serve. To serve cut waffles into quarter sections. Place strawberry halves on each serving. Spoon whipped cream on top. Serve immediately. Makes about 2 waffles or 4 servings.

Chocolate Waffle Ice Cream Sandwiches

Once upon a time there was a king named A-B-A whose kingdom rested on a little cloud, sandwiched between two big mountains. This cloud sheltered the town below from the hot sun and kept it pleasant the year round for everyone. From time to time King A-B-A would look down from his lofty cloud to make sure everything was alright. It was a wonderful place to be! And so as a gesture of thanks, the townspeople created this sandwich and called it an A-B-A, in his honor. And, of course, it is a wonderful thing to eat!

4 ounces semisweet chocolate
1/4 cup butter
2 cups all-purpose flour
1/2 cup sugar
1-1/2 tablespoons baking powder
1/2 teaspoon baking soda
2 tablespoons unsweetened cocoa powder

2 eggs, separated
3/4 cup milk
1/2 cup dairy sour cream
1/2 teaspoon vanilla extract
1/4 teaspoon cream of tartar
Vegetable shortening or oil for grids
1 quart vanilla ice cream

In a small saucepan or double boiler melt chocolate and butter together over low heat, stirring occasionally. Preheat waffle iron. In a medium-size bowl sift together flour, sugar, baking powder, baking soda and cocoa powder. In a large bowl beat together egg yolks, milk, sour cream and vanilla. Gradually stir in flour mixture. Beat until smooth. Stir in melted chocolate and butter. In a small bowl whip egg whites and cream of tartar until soft peaks are formed. Fold into batter. Lightly brush hot grids with shortening or oil. Pour enough batter to fill two-thirds of the waffle iron. Cook until crisp and a rich brown. Cool finished waffles on a rack. Cut into 2-inch rounds with a cookie cutter. Gently spoon about 3 tablespoons of vanilla ice cream onto half of the waffle rounds. Place the remaining rounds on top of the ice cream, creating a sandwich. Wipe off any ice cream that melts over the sides. Wrap each one individually in foil and place in the freezer 1 hour. Remaining sandwiches will stay fresh in the freezer several days. Makes about 4 waffles or 12 sandwiches.

Papaya Waffles with Raspberry Sorbet

These waffles have an exotic, light flavor that is uniquely their own. With the sweet essence of papaya coupled with the snappy Raspberry Sorbet this waffle ensemble is deceivingly good.

1 ripe papaya, peeled, seeds removed, cut into
  2-inch pieces
1-1/2 cups all-purpose flour
1 tablespoon baking powder
1/2 teaspoon baking soda
1/4 cup sugar
2 eggs, separated
3/4 cup papaya nectar
1/4 cup plain low-fat yogurt
1-1/4 teaspoons vanilla extract

1 tablespoon fresh lime juice
3 tablespoons vegetable oil
Vegetable shortening or oil for grids

RASPBERRY SORBET:

1-1/2 cups water
1 (1/4-oz.) envelope unflavored gelatin
1 (12-oz.) package raspberries, frozen, thawed
1/2 cup superfine sugar
1 tablespoon fresh lemon juice
1 egg white

Prepare Raspberry Sorbet at least 9 hours ahead. Preheat waffle iron. Preheat oven to 250°F (120°C). Place papaya pieces in a large bowl and mash with a fork. In a medium-size bowl sift together flour, baking powder, baking soda and sugar. Add egg yolks, papaya nectar, yogurt, vanilla, lime juice and oil to the bowl with the mashed papaya. Gradually stir in flour mixture. Beat until smooth. In a small bowl whip egg whites until soft peaks are formed. Fold into batter. Lightly brush hot grids with shortening or oil. Pour enough batter to fill two-thirds of the waffle iron. Cook until crisp and golden-brown. While the waffles are cooking, remove the Raspberry Sorbet from the freezer. Keep finished waffles warm in the oven on a rack until ready to serve. Repeat with the remaining batter. To serve cut waffles into quarter sections. With an ice cream scoop make Raspberry Sorbet balls and place on top of each section. Serve immediately. Makes about 3 waffles or 4 servings.

RASPBERRY SORBET

In a small bowl combine 1 cup of the water and gelatin. Let stand 10 minutes. In a small saucepan slowly warm raspberries over low heat until small bubbles form around the edges. Stir in remaining 1/2 cup of water, sugar, lemon juice and gelatin mixture. Stir constantly until all ingredients are combined and sugar is dissolved. Transfer to a medium-size bowl and freeze 1 hour. Remove frozen mixture from freezer. With an electric mixer beat frozen mixture until smooth and foamy. In a small bowl whip the egg white until soft peaks are formed. Add to raspberry mixture. Beat 30 seconds. Freeze 8 hours. Makes about 2-1/2 cups.

Pumpkin Cheesecake Waffles

You no longer have to wait until Autumn to enjoy the taste of pumpkin cheesecake. This waffle is so good you'll be expecting the leaves on the trees to change even in Spring!

1 cup all-purpose flour
1/2 cup sugar
1-1/2 tablespoons baking powder
1/2 teaspoon baking soda
1/4 teaspoon salt
1/2 teaspoon ground cinnamon
1/8 teaspoon ground cloves
1/8 teaspoon ground ginger
1 cup canned pumpkin puree

1 (8-oz.) package cream cheese, softened
1/4 cup ricotta cheese
2 eggs
1/4 cup dairy sour cream
1/2 teaspoon vanilla extract
1/3 cup vegetable oil
Vegetable shortening or oil for grids
1 cup whipping cream
1/4 cup sugar

Preheat waffle iron. Preheat oven to 250°F (120°C). In a medium-size bowl sift together flour, the 1/2 cup sugar, baking powder, baking soda, salt and spices. In a large bowl beat together pumpkin puree, cream cheese, ricotta cheese, eggs, sour cream, vanilla and oil. Gradually stir in flour mixture. Beat until smooth. Lightly brush hot grids with shortening or oil. Pour enough batter to fill two-thirds of the waffle iron. Cook until crisp and golden-brown. While the waffles are cooking, in a small bowl whip together cream and the 1/4 cup sugar until soft peaks are formed. Keep refrigerated until ready to serve. Keep finished waffles warm in the oven on a rack until ready to serve. Repeat with the remaining batter. To serve, cut waffles into quarter sections. Serve hot with a spoonful of whipped cream on top. Makes about 2 waffles or 4 servings.

Low-Calorie Raspberry Waffles with Clouds

Sounds inviting? Well it is. Here's a rich and flavorful dessert that is light as a cloud and low in calories. How heavenly.

1-1/2 cups all-purpose flour
2 tablespoons granulated sugar
1/4 teaspoon baking soda
1/4 teaspoon salt
2 eggs, separated
2 tablespoons vegetable oil
2 cups natural raspberry sparkling drink
1/4 teaspoon cream of tartar
Shortening or oil grids
2 cups sliced fresh strawberries

Powdered sugar

CLOUD TOPPING:

4 egg whites, room temperature
1 teaspoon cream of tartar
Pinch of salt
1/3 cup powdered sugar
1 tablespoon grated grapefruit zest
1/2 teaspoon vanilla extract
1 tablespoon orange liqueur (optional)

In a medium-size bowl sift together flour, granulated sugar, baking soda and salt. In a large bowl beat together egg yolks and oil. Stir in raspberry drink. Gradually stir in flour mixture. With an electric mixer on low speed beat until smooth about 30 seconds. Do not over beat. In a small bowl whip egg whites and cream of tartar until soft peaks are formed. Fold into batter. Cover. Let batter rise 2 hours. Preheat waffle iron. Lightly brush hot grids with shortening or oil. Pour enough batter to fill two-thirds of the waffle iron. Cook until crisp and golden-brown. While the waffles are cooking, prepare Cloud Topping. Let finished waffles cool on a rack. Repeat with the remaining batter. To serve, cut waffles into quarter or half sections. Preheat broiler. Place strawberry slices on top of each section. Place a scoop of Cloud Topping on top of the strawberries. Place under broiler 1 to 2 minutes or until the top of the egg whites turns light brown. Sprinkle powdered sugar through a fine sieve over the top. Serve immediately. Makes about 3 waffles or 4 servings.

CLOUD TOPPING

In a medium-size bowl combine egg whites and cream of tartar. With an electric mixer beat egg whites on low speed 30 seconds. Increase speed to high and beat an additional 30 seconds or until foamy. Gradually add salt, sugar, grapefruit zest, vanilla and orange liqueur, if using. Continue to whip on high until stiff peaks are formed. Makes about 1 cup.

Fruit Tart on a Gingersnap Waffle

This warm, snappy waffle under a traditional tart filling adds an entirely new dimension that will surprise and delight even the most selective pastry chef!

12 (2-1/2-inch) graham cracker squares
3/4 cup all-purpose flour
1/2 teaspoon baking powder
1/2 teaspoon baking soda
1-1/2 tablespoons ground ginger
2 eggs, separated
1 cup milk
1/3 cup packed dark brown sugar
2 tablespoons butter, melted, cooled
1/2 teaspoon vanilla extract
Vegetable shortening or oil for grids
1 cup sliced fresh strawberries
1/2 cup sliced kiwifruit
1 cup fresh blackberries

CREAM-CHEESE FILLING:

1/2 cup (4 ounces) cream cheese, softened
1/4 cup butter, softened
1/2 teaspoon vanilla extract
1/4 cup sugar
1/4 cup whipping cream
1/2 teaspoon fresh lemon juice

APRICOT GLAZE:

1-1/2 cups apricot preserves
1/4 cup hot water

Prepare Cream-Cheese Filling and refrigerate. In a blender or food processor fitted with the metal blade process graham crackers until they form fine crumbs. Preheat waffle iron. In a medium-size bowl whisk together graham cracker crumbs, all-purpose flour, baking powder, baking soda and ginger. In a large bowl beat together egg yolks, milk, brown sugar, butter and vanilla. Gradually stir in flour mixture. Beat until smooth. In a small bowl whip egg whites until soft peaks are formed. Fold into batter. Lightly brush hot grids with shortening or oil. Pour enough batter to fill two-thirds of the waffle iron. Cook until crisp and a rich brown. Be careful not to overcook. While the waffles are cooking, prepare the Apricot Glaze. Let finished waffles cool on a rack. Repeat with the remaining batter. To serve break waffles into quarter sections. Spread a layer of chilled Cream-Cheese Filling on one quarter section, alternate strawberry slices, kiwifruit slices and blackberries. Pour 2 to 3 tablespoons of the Apricot Glaze over the top. Serve immediately. Makes about 3 waffles or 4 servings.

CREAM-CHEESE FILLING

In a medium-size bowl blend together cream cheese, butter, vanilla, sugar, cream and lemon juice. Keep refrigerated until ready to serve. Makes about 1-1/2 cups.

APRICOT GLAZE

In a small saucepan combine apricot preserves and water. Warm over low heat until small bubbles appear around the edges, stirring occasionally. Do not boil. Keep warm until ready to serve. Makes about 1 cup.

Mint-Chocolate Waffles with Creme de Menthe Topping

Minty, chocolatey, creamy—sinfully irresistible. One of the best ways to finish off a delicious dinner.

4 ounces semisweet chocolate
1/4 cup butter
1-1/4 cups all-purpose flour
1/3 cup sugar
1 tablespoon baking powder
1/2 teaspoon baking soda
2 tablespoons unsweetened cocoa powder
2 eggs, separated
1/2 cup milk
1/2 cup dairy sour cream

1/4 cup vegetable oil
2 teaspoons peppermint extract
Vegetable shortening or oil for grids
1 quart chocolate-mint ice cream
Mint sprigs for garnish

CREME DE MENTHE TOPPING:

1 cup whipping cream
1 tablespoon Creme de Menthe liqueur
2 tablespoons superfine sugar

Preheat waffle iron. Preheat oven to 250°F (120°C). In a small saucepan or double boiler melt chocolate and butter together over low heat. In a medium-size bowl sift together flour, sugar, baking powder, baking soda and cocoa powder. In a large bowl beat together egg yolks, milk, sour cream, oil and mint extract. Gradually stir in flour mixture, melted chocolate and butter. Beat until smooth. In a small bowl whip egg whites until soft peaks are formed. Fold into batter. Lightly brush hot grids with shortening or oil. Cook until crisp and a rich brown. While the waffles are cooking prepare the Creme de Menthe Topping. Keep finished waffles warm in the oven on a rack until ready to serve. To serve, cut waffles into quarter sections. Spoon Creme de Menthe Topping on top. Serve with chocolate-mint ice cream on the side. Garnish with mint sprigs. Makes about 2 waffles or 4 servings.

CREME DE MENTHE TOPPING

In a medium-size bowl combine whipping cream, liqueur and sugar. Beat until soft peaks are formed. Keep refrigerated until ready to serve. Makes about 2 cups.

Oreo® Cookie Waffles

America's favorite cookie is transformed into a totally awesome dessert waffle! Enjoy it plain or with vanilla ice cream. And of course you can dunk them in milk if you like.

1-1/2 cups all-purpose flour
1 tablespoon baking powder
1/4 teaspoon baking soda
1/2 cup sugar
2 eggs
3/4 cup milk

1/2 cup whipping cream
1/2 teaspoon vanilla extract
3 tablespoons vegetable oil
1 cup broken Oreo cookies
Vegetable shortening or oil for grids
1 quart vanilla ice cream

Preheat waffle iron. Preheat oven to 250°F (120°C). In a medium-size bowl sift together flour, baking powder, baking soda and sugar. In a large bowl beat together eggs, milk, cream, vanilla and oil. Gradually stir in flour mixture. Beat until smooth. Stir in Oreo cookie pieces. Lightly brush hot grids with shortening or oil. Ladle enough batter to fill one-half of each section on the waffle iron. (Do not overfill.) Cook until crisp and golden-brown. Keep finished waffles warm in the oven on a rack until ready to serve. Repeat with the remaining batter. Serve waffles sections hot with a scoop of ice cream. Serve immediately. Makes about 12 sections or 4 servings.

Cheesecake on a Graham Cracker Waffle
with Strawberry Sauce

This is a novel way to make cheesecake because the crust is replaced with a waffle. Your guests may do a double take at this crust with grids, but with one bite they'll be locked into the taste.

18 (2-1/2-inch) graham cracker squares
3/4 cup all-purpose flour
1 teaspoon baking powder
1/4 teaspoon baking soda
1 teaspoon ground cinnamon
2 eggs, separated
1/4 cup packed dark brown sugar
2 tablespoons vegetable oil
1 cup club soda
1 egg white (from cheesecake)
1/8 teaspoon cream of tartar
Vegetable shortening or oil for grids

CHEESECAKE:

24 ounces cream cheese, softened
3/4 cup sugar

2 tablespoons all-purpose flour
1 teaspoon vanilla extract
1/2 teaspoon almond extract
1 teaspoon fresh lemon juice
3 eggs
1 egg yolk
2 tablespoons whipping cream
2 tablespoons dairy sour cream

STRAWBERRY SAUCE:

2 cups strawberries, fresh or frozen, thawed,
   drained
1 tablespoon fresh lemon juice
1 tablespoon vanilla extract
1/3 cup powdered sugar

Prepare Cheesecake. In a blender or food processor fitted with the metal blade process graham crackers until they form fine crumbs. In a large bowl whisk together graham cracker crumbs, all-purpose flour, baking powder, baking soda and cinnamon. In a small bowl beat together egg yolks, brown sugar and oil. Gradually stir in egg mixture and club soda to flour mixture. Stir until blended. Do not beat. In a small bowl whip the 3 egg whites and cream of tartar until soft peaks are formed. Fold into batter. Chill batter 1 hour. Preheat waffle iron. Lightly brush hot grids with shortening or oil. Pour enough batter to fill two-thirds of the waffle iron. Cook until crisp and golden-brown. While the waffles are cooking, prepare the Strawberry Sauce. Let finished waffle cool on a rack. Repeat with the remaining batter. To serve, cut chilled cheesecake into 6 slices and place one slice diagonally on each cooled waffle section. Pour a ribbon of Strawberry Sauce over the top of each serving. Makes about 3 waffles or 6 servings.

CHEESECAKE

Preheat oven to 350°F (175°C). In a large bowl beat together cream cheese, sugar, flour, vanilla, almond extract and lemon juice. Beat in eggs and egg yolk, one at a time. Add whipping cream and sour cream. Beat until all ingredients are blended. Pour into greased 9-inch round springform pan. Bake 40 to 45 minutes or until a pick inserted in the center comes out clean. Cool on a rack. Refrigerate 2 hours before serving.

STRAWBERRY SAUCE

In a blender or food processor fitted with the metal blade combine strawberries, lemon juice, vanilla and powdered sugar. Process until smooth. Keep refrigerated until ready to serve. Before serving transfer to a container with an easy pour spout. Makes about 1-1/2 cups.

Eggnog Waffles

Even though eggnog is traditionally served in a mug, it can magically become a delightful holiday waffle, but only if you believe in Santa Claus! Happy Holidays!

2 cups all-purpose flour
1 tablespoon baking powder
1/2 teaspoon baking soda
3 tablespoons sugar
1 teaspoon ground nutmeg
1-1/2 cups eggnog
1/2 cup plain low-fat yogurt

1/2 cup milk
2 eggs, separated
1/4 cup butter, melted, cooled
Vegetable shortening or oil for grids
1 cup butter, melted
1/2 cup maple syrup, warmed

Preheat waffle iron. Preheat oven to 250°F (120°C). In a medium-size bowl sift together flour, baking powder, baking soda, sugar and nutmeg. In a large bowl beat together eggnog, yogurt, milk, egg yolks and the 1/4 cup butter. Gradually stir in flour mixture. Beat until smooth. In a small bowl whip egg whites until soft peaks are formed. Fold into batter. Lightly brush hot grids with shortening or oil. Pour enough batter to fill two-thirds of the waffle iron. Cook until crisp and golden-brown. Keep finished waffles warm in the oven on a rack until ready to serve. Repeat with the remaining batter. Serve waffles hot with the 1 cup melted butter and maple syrup. Makes about 4 waffles or 4 servings.

Fruitcake Waffles

These waffles are cut into festive little round fruitcakes that are terrific around the holidays. Quick to prepare and easy to serve, they are ideal for when unexpected carolers arrive at your doorstep.

1 cup all-purpose flour
1/2 cup whole-wheat flour
1-1/2 tablespoons baking powder
1/2 teaspoon baking soda
1/2 teaspoon unsweetened cocoa powder
3/4 cup sugar
1/2 teaspoon ground cloves
1/2 teaspoon ground cinnamon
3/4 teaspoon ground nutmeg
2 eggs
1 cup buttermilk
1/2 cup dry sherry
1/2 cup butter, melted, cooled
1/2 teaspoon vanilla extract

1/2 teaspoon almond extract
1 tablespoon dark molasses
1 teaspoon grated lemon zest
1/4 cup golden raisins
1/2 cup walnuts
3/4 cup fruitcake mix
Vegetable shortening or oil for grids

ORANGE GLAZE:

1/2 cup orange juice
3 tablespoons powdered sugar
1 tablespoon grated orange zest
1 tablespoon brandy

Preheat waffle iron. Preheat oven to 250°F (120°C). In a medium-size bowl sift together all-purpose flour, whole-wheat flour, baking powder, baking soda, cocoa powder, sugar, cloves, cinnamon and nutmeg. In a large bowl beat together eggs, buttermilk, sherry, butter, vanilla, almond extract and molasses. Gradually stir in flour mixture. Beat until smooth. Stir in lemon zest, raisins, walnuts and fruitcake mix. Lightly brush hot grids with shortening or oil. Pour enough batter to fill two-thirds of the waffle iron. Cook until crisp and a rich brown. While the waffles are cooking, prepare the Orange Glaze. Keep finished waffles warm in the oven on a rack until ready to serve. Repeat with the remaining batter. To serve, cut waffles into 2-inch rounds with a cookie cutter. Drizzle Orange Glaze over the top. Makes about 3 waffles or 20 rounds.

ORANGE GLAZE

In a small bowl combine orange juice, powdered sugar, orange zest and brandy. Set aside. Stir before serving. Makes about 1/2 cup.

Bosco's Delights

These chocolate waffles are named after our chocolate labrador who is the number one taster at our house. But it was with the true chocolate lover in mind that their rich flavor was created. Of course, if you eat all of them, you too could end up in the dog house!

3 ounces semisweet chocolate
1/4 cup butter
2 cups all-purpose flour
1/3 cup sugar
1 tablespoon baking powder
1/2 teaspoon baking soda
2 tablespoons unsweetened cocoa powder
2 eggs, separated
1/2 cup milk
1/2 cup dairy sour cream

1/2 teaspoon vanilla extract
Vegetable shortening or oil for grids
1 quart vanilla ice cream

CHOCOLATE SAUCE:

1 cup semisweet chocolate chips
1/4 cup butter
1/2 cup whipping cream
1/3 cup sugar
1 teaspoon vanilla extract
1 tablespoon unsweetened cocoa powder

Preheat waffle iron. Preheat oven to 250°F (120°C). In a small saucepan or double boiler melt chocolate and butter over low heat, stirring occasionally. In a medium-size bowl sift together flour, sugar, baking powder, baking soda and cocoa powder. In a large bowl beat together egg yolks, milk, sour cream and vanilla. Gradually stir in flour mixture and melted chocolate and butter. Beat until smooth. In a small bowl whip egg whites until soft peaks are formed. Fold into batter. Lightly brush hot grids with shortening or oil. Pour enough batter to fill two-thirds of the waffle iron. Cook until crisp and a rich brown. While the waffles are cooking, prepare the Chocolate Sauce. Keep finished waffles warm in the oven on a rack until ready to serve. To serve, cut waffles into quarter or half sections. Spoon a scoop of ice cream on top and cover with hot Chocolate Sauce. Makes about 2 waffles or 4 servings.

CHOCOLATE SAUCE

In a medium-size saucepan or double-boiler melt chocolate and butter over low heat. Stir in cream, sugar, vanilla and cocoa powder. Do not boil. Stir occasionally for 3 minutes. Simmer. Keep warm until ready to serve. Makes about 1 cup.

Peanut Butter Fudge Waffles

Wow! When these two great tastes are blended together, they drive people crazy because they are so good. And these waffles are no exception.

2 ounces unsweetened chocolate
1/3 cup butter
1-1/2 cups all-purpose flour
1 tablespoon baking powder
1 tablespoon unsweetened cocoa powder
1/2 teaspoon salt
1 cup granulated sugar
3/4 cup milk
1/4 cup whipping cream
2 eggs

1/2 teaspoon almond extract
1/2 teaspoon vanilla extract
1 tablespoon molasses
3/4 cup smooth peanut butter
1/4 cup semisweet chocolate chips
1/3 cup unsalted peanuts, skinned, chopped
Vegetable shortening or oil for grids
Powdered sugar
Chocolate ice cream

Preheat waffle iron. Preheat oven to 250°F (120°C). In a small, heavy saucepan or double boiler melt chocolate and butter over low heat, stirring occasionally. In a medium-size bowl sift together flour, baking powder, cocoa powder, salt and granulated sugar. In a large bowl beat together milk, cream, eggs, almond extract, vanilla and molasses. Gradually stir in flour mixture, melted chocolate and butter and peanut butter. Beat until smooth. Stir in chocolate chips and peanuts. Batter will be thick. Lightly brush hot grids with shortening or oil. Pour enough batter to fill one-half of each section of the waffle iron. Cook until crisp and a rich brown. Be careful not to overcook. Keep finished waffles warm in the oven on a rack until ready to serve. Repeat with the remaining batter. Serve waffles hot with powdered sugar and a scoop of ice cream on the side. Makes about 3 waffles or 12 servings.

Lime Waffles with Papaya Sorbet

This light waffle and sorbet combination is extraordinary. And with this easy way to prepare sorbet without an ice cream maker, you can create a dessert that is magnificent!

1-1/2 cups all-purpose flour
1 tablespoon baking powder
1/2 teaspoon baking soda
1/4 cup superfine sugar
1/4 cup milk
1/4 cup half and half
1/2 cup fresh lime juice
1/2 teaspoon vanilla extract
2 eggs, separated
2 tablespoons vegetable oil

1 tablespoon grated lime zest
Vegetable shortening or oil for grids

PAPAYA SORBET:

1-1/2 cups water
1 (1/4-oz.) envelope unflavored gelatin
2 ripe papayas, halved, seeds removed
1/2 cup superfine sugar
2 tablespoons fresh lime juice
1 tablespoon grated lemon zest
2 egg whites
1/8 teaspoon cream of tartar

Prepare Papaya Sorbet at least 9 hours before serving. Preheat waffle iron. Preheat oven to 250°F (120°C). In a medium-size bowl sift together flour, baking powder, baking soda and sugar. In a large bowl beat together milk, half and half, lime juice, vanilla, egg yolks and oil. Gradually stir in flour mixture. Beat until smooth. Stir in lime zest. In a small bowl whip egg whites until soft peaks are formed. Fold into batter. Lightly brush hot grids with shortening or oil. Pour enough batter to fill two-thirds of the waffle iron. Cook until crisp and golden-brown. While the waffles are cooking, remove Papaya Sorbet from the freezer. Keep finished waffles warm in the oven on a rack until ready to serve. Repeat with the remaining batter. To serve, place a scoop of Papaya Sorbet on top of each waffle. Serve immediately. Makes about 4 waffles or 4 servings.

PAPAYA SORBET

In a small bowl combine 1/2 cup of the water and gelatin. Stir to dissolve. Let stand 10 minutes. In a blender or food processor fitted with the metal blade process papaya until smooth. Transfer papaya puree to a medium-size saucepan. Warm slowly over low heat. Stir in remaining 1 cup water, sugar, lime juice, lemon zest and gelatin mixture. Simmer 5 minutes, stirring occasionally. Transfer to a shallow bowl. Freeze 1 hour. Remove frozen papaya mixture from the freezer. With an electric mixer beat mixture 1 minute or until foamy. In a small bowl whip egg whites with cream of tartar until soft peaks are formed. Add to papaya mixture and beat on high speed 30 seconds. Cover. Freeze 8 hours. Makes about 3 cups.

Sweet Rice Pudding Waffles

Just like a dish of creamy rice pudding you order at a diner, this innovative twist on an old favorite is great with just a little whipped cream on top.

1-1/3 cups water
1/2 cup uncooked rice
1-1/2 cups all-purpose flour
1-1/2 tablespoons baking powder
1/4 teaspoon salt
1/2 cup sugar
1/2 teaspoon ground cinnamon

3 eggs, separated
1-1/4 cups milk
1/2 cup raisins
Vegetable shortening or oil for grids
1 cup whipping cream
1/4 cup sugar

In a medium-size saucepan bring water to a boil. Stir in rice. Reduce heat and simmer until all the water is absorbed 15 to 20 minutes. Preheat waffle iron. Preheat oven to 250°F (120°C). In a medium-size bowl sift together all-purpose flour, baking powder, salt, the 1/2 cup sugar and cinnamon. In a large bowl beat together egg yolks and milk. Gradually stir in flour mixture. Beat until smooth. Stir in cooked rice and raisins. In a small bowl whip egg whites until soft peaks are formed. Fold into batter. Lightly brush hot grids with shortening or oil. Pour enough batter to fill two-thirds of the waffle iron. Cook until crisp and golden-brown. While the waffles are cooking, in a small bowl whip together cream and the 1/4 cup sugar until soft peaks are formed. Keep refrigerated until ready to serve. Keep finished waffles warm in the oven on a rack until ready to serve. Repeat with the remaining batter. To serve, break waffles into quarter sections. Serve hot with whipped cream on top. Makes about 3 waffles or 12 servings.

Index

Comparison to Metric Measure

When You Know	Symbol	Multiply By	To Find	Symbol
teaspoons	tsp	5.0	milliliters	ml
tablespoons	tbsp	15.0	milliliters	ml
fluid ounces	fl. oz.	30.0	milliliters	ml
cups	c	0.24	liters	l
pints	pt.	0.47	liters	l
quarts	qt.	0.95	liters	l
ounces	oz.	28.0	grams	g
pounds	lb.	0.45	kilograms	kg
Fahrenheit	F	5/9 (after subtracting 32)	Celsius	C

Liquid Measure to Milliliters

1/4 teaspoon	=	1.25 milliliters
1/2 teaspoon	=	2.5 milliliters
3/4 teaspoon	=	3.75 milliliters
1 teaspoon	=	5.0 milliliters
1-1/4 teaspoons	=	6.25 milliliters
1-1/2 teaspoons	=	7.5 milliliters
1-3/4 teaspoons	=	8.75 milliliters
2 teaspoons	=	10.0 milliliters
1 tablespoon	=	15.0 milliliters
2 tablespoons	=	30.0 milliliters

Fahrenheit to Celsius

F	C
200—205	95
220—225	105
245—250	120
275	135
300—305	150
325—330	165
345—350	175
370—375	190
400—405	205
425—430	220
445—450	230
470—475	245
500	260

Liquid Measure to Liters

1/4 cup	=	0.06 liters
1/2 cup	=	0.12 liters
3/4 cup	=	0.18 liters
1 cup	=	0.24 liters
1-1/4 cups	=	0.3 liters
1-1/2 cups	=	0.36 liters
2 cups	=	0.48 liters
2-1/2 cups	=	0.6 liters
3 cups	=	0.72 liters
3-1/2 cups	=	0.84 liters
4 cups	=	0.96 liters
4-1/2 cups	=	1.08 liters
5 cups	=	1.2 liters
5-1/2 cups	=	1.32 liters